How to Teach
so Students
ReMeMBeR

Marilee Sprenger

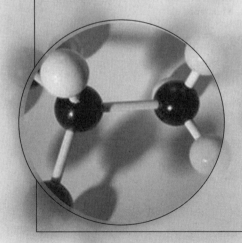

Association for Supervision and Curriculum Development
Alexandria, Virginia, USA

Association for Supervision and Curriculum Development
1703 N. Beauregard St. • Alexandria, VA 22311-1714 USA
Phone: 800-933-2723 or 703-578-9600 • Fax: 703-575-5400
Web site: www.ascd.org • E-mail: member@ascd.org
Author guidelines: www.ascd.org/write

Gene R. Carter, *Executive Director;* Nancy Modrak, *Director of Publishing;* Julie Houtz, *Director of Book Editing & Production;* Deborah Siegel, *Project Manager;* Media Plus Design, *Graphic Designer;* Cynthia Stock, *Typesetter;* Tracey A. Franklin, *Production Manager*

ASCD publications present a variety of viewpoints. The views expressed or implied in this book should not be interpreted as official positions of the Association.

All Web links in this book are correct as of the publication date below but may have become inactive or otherwise modified since that time. If you notice a deactivated or changed link, please e-mail books@ascd.org with the words "Link Update" in the subject line. In your message, please specify the Web link, the book title, and the page number on which the link appears.

Paperback ISBN: 1-4166-0152-X • ASCD product #105016 • List Price: 25.95 ($19.95 ASCD member price, direct from ASCD only)   s5/05
e-books ($25.95): retail PDF ISBN: 1-4166-0288-7 • netLibrary ISBN 1-4166-0286-0 • ebrary ISBN 1-4166-0287-9

Quantity discounts for the paperback book: 10–49 copies, 10%; 50+ copies, 15%; for 500 or more copies, call 800-933-2723, ext. 5634, or 703-575-5634.

Library of Congress Cataloging-in-Publication Data

Sprenger, Marilee, 1949–
   How to teach so students remember / Marilee Sprenger.
      p. cm.
   Includes bibliographical references and index.
   ISBN 1-4166-0152-X (alk. paper)
  1. Teaching. 2. Learning. 3. Memory. I. Title.

   LB1027.S685 2005
   371.102—dc22

                 2005000166

10 09 08 07 06 05   12 11 10 9 8 7 6 5 4 3 2 1

To Mom, Dad, Sande, Linda, and Jeff,
who are the keepers of my childhood memories.

To Evelyn, Ellyn, Carolyn, and Jennifer,
who remind me to remember (when they remember to remind me).

To Sally, Gail, Nancy, Jan, Lori, Cindy, and Penny,
who work with me to expand my knowledge and my memory.

To Donna, Mary Jane, and Betty,
who enrich my brain and challenge my memory.

To Scott, Josh, and Marnie,
who make every moment of my life worth remembering.

121198

How to Teach so Students REMEMBER

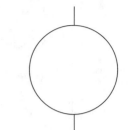

Acknowledgments

An incredible group of friends, researchers, and colleagues invested much time and energy in creating this book. Many memory researchers are working diligently to find answers to the various questions we all have about how our memories work or why they don't. I want to thank Daniel Schacter for his research and his wonderful publications, for the time he devoted to examining the seven steps, and for his encouragement.

The work done by Bob Marzano, Jane E. Pollack, and Debra Pickering has contributed greatly to the pursuit of higher student achievement. We are all better-informed educators as a result. My friends and colleagues at Two Rivers Professional Development Center provide constant encouragement. I want especially to thank Gail Owen for her affirmation and her time.

I am grateful to the people at ASCD, especially Carolyn Pool and Scott Willis, for their support, encouragement, and cooperation.

I am indebted to all "my kids," the students who taught me so much, and to the thousands of teachers whose lives have touched mine.

Finally, I want to thank my mother, Mollie Broms, and my husband, Scott, for reading my manuscripts and offering suggestions and support.

Introduction

I am sitting across from two of my students. Bobby is probably the best young chess player I have ever known. He also is a very good student. He wants to be a doctor just like his dad and his mom. Cory, in contrast, doesn't care much about school and spends most of his time on his skateboard. He is the best skateboarder I have ever seen. I don't think Cory knows where his dad is or what he does; his mother has a day care in her home. I am concerned that he is not learning very much. I am with them to see whether I can discover how they learn.

"Cory, how did you get to be so good at skateboarding?" I ask.

"Practice," he replies.

"OK, how did you get interested in it?"

"I dunno," he responds. "I think I just seen this guy on a board doin' all these tricks, and I thought it was cool. I asked my brother to get me a board, and he did."

"So, you saw this guy. You bought a board. And you practiced?"

"Yeah. I thought I could be good."

"Thanks, Cory. How about you, Bobby? How did you get involved with chess?" I ask him.

"I saw the movie Searching for Bobby Fischer. I thought it was cool the way they made their moves so fast. My dad has a chessboard in his office at home. I started reading about chess and practicing," Bobby says.

"Are you hoping to be another Bobby Fisher?" I want to know.

"Maybe," he replies shyly.

"OK, boys, I want to know the process. You saw somebody do it. You practiced until you were good. Is that it?"

Cory nods. "If you want to be good, you have to think about it and picture it in your mind. And you gotta practice. A lot."

"How do you know when you've got it right?" I ask.

"When you don't bang your knees and elbows or break your wrist!" Cory laughs.

"With chess, you find out when you win or lose," Bobby offers.

"OK. Let's look at the steps again. You find out about it. You think about it. You try it. You get feedback by either losing a game or getting hurt. You practice until you get it right. Is that it?"

"Then you compete," Bobby says. Cory nods.

"How do you prepare for a competition?" I ask both boys.

"I review all my moves. In my head and on the board," Bobby responds.

"Yup. I do the same," Cory adds. "I go over and over my jumps. And I try to make up my own moves. Ya gotta get creative to win at boarding."

"It's kind of like that with chess, too," Bobby begins. "My dad will make some unconventional moves, and I have to counter those moves. It's harder to win against an amateur sometimes because they don't follow the usual playing patterns."

"So, you practice until you're perfect, and then you practice the unexpected?" I ask.

"Yup. That's it. Anything else?" Cory seems anxious to leave.

"One more thing. When you compete, even though you're prepared, are there any specific factors that affect your performance?"

Bobby speaks first. "Sometimes I get really nervous, and I can't see the moves in my head. I have to try to relax. It helps if I have been able to practice at the place where I compete. Usually I get that opportunity."

"Yeah," Cory breaks in. "I was trying to do a hardflip at this skate park in Chicago, and I didn't know the place at all. It took me three times to get it right. When I fell the second time, I looked at my brother and remembered how he told me to do it."

"Thanks, boys. You've helped me a great deal. I'll see you both in class." I smile as they leave.

These boys shared with me the secret, the system. Two very different individuals who follow the same learning pattern—one using it for a physical skill, the other for a mental one. They followed the identical steps. And their system made perfect sense with the way the brain learns and remembers.

This book is not an attempt to teach the biology of the brain. Many excellent books are available that do that. This book describes a seven-step process for us to store pertinent information in long-term memory and then to be able to access those memories in many different situations. Creating accessible memories takes time.

Some of you will be very familiar with the brain terminology, but for those of you who are not, Appendix A provides a "brain briefing." Most of you will be more interested in the steps themselves. I urge you to examine the memory processes as they are explained. Being able to articulate the reasons why something works is helpful in spreading the word: Brain-compatible teaching works.

I believe very much in Stephen Covey's (1989) habit of beginning with the end in mind. In *The Seven Habits of Highly Effective People*, he says, "To begin with the end in mind means to start with a clear understanding of your destination. It means to know where you're going so that you better understand where you are now so that the steps you take are always in the right direction" (p. 98). Teaching for memory will be successful if you are clear about what your students need to remember. To make the journey exciting, productive, and memorable is what this book is about.

I make several assumptions as I write this book:

- The teacher who is teaching for memory and transfer determines first what needs to be measured.

- This teacher then creates the assessment.

- This teacher gives students a clear target.

- This teacher is attempting to plan learning experiences and instruction that will clearly lead students to the target.

- This teacher is revealing important information to the students that they will be able to use in the real world.

- This teacher has created a brain-compatible classroom.

- Even though memorization may play some role in what is taught, this teacher is teaching for conceptual understanding.

Before You Take a Step, Step Back

I give my participants what I call "The Marshmallow Test." No, it's not the one that was done at Stanford University to determine impulse control. For that study, four-year-olds were offered two marshmallows if they could wait for someone to return from an errand. If they could not wait, they were to be given one marshmallow right away (Goleman, 1995). My test is different. When my workshop participants arrive, sign in, and are seated, I pass out one marshmallow to each. I ask them not to eat it. When everyone has a marshmallow, I announce, "This is really a simple task. All you need to do is throw the marshmallow in the bucket. I'm sure everyone can do that. Ready? Set? Go!"

They all sit motionless. One or two will ask, "Where's the bucket? How can we throw it in the bucket if there is no bucket?"

I smile and say, "Oh, so you're saying you need a target?" They all nod. I pull a large bucket out from behind my chair. I hold the bucket and walk around. "OK, here's the bucket. Ready? Set? Go!" A few fling their marshmallows at the bucket, but most sit still.

"What's the problem?" I ask.

"Quit moving! It's too hard to hit a moving target!" some say.

"So, not only do you want a clear target, but you want it to be stationary?" I ask.

They agree. I put the bucket down and again say, "Ready? Set? Go!" Marshmallows fly through the air. A few go in the bucket, but most miss.

"Would you be willing to let this assessment go on your permanent record?" I ask.

They all say no. It wouldn't be fair. They didn't get to practice.

And this is how the discussion on providing clear targets begins: with expectations for our students. It further extends to the amount of practice that should be provided, the use of different instructional strategies, and plenty of feedback. After examining the state standards for this group and spending the day talking about aligning our instruction, review, and assessment, I send the teachers attending my workshop home with their first assignment: target practice. They are to define what concepts they want their students to understand and share those with them. The target should be written on the board each day so that both the students and the teacher are clear about what is expected.

"Take Two Steps Forward."
"Mother, May I?"
"No, You May Not!"

This approach is called *backward design* (Wiggins & McTighe, 1998), *beginning with the end in mind* (Covey, 1989), or *developing clear targets* (Stiggins, 2001). The point is that we want to match our assessment and instruction to our learning goals. To accomplish this, we must choose and create the assessments *before* we begin the instructional process. This method provides intentional learning. If your students know from the beginning what the intentions are, they can purposely learn based on the clarity of your targets.

I'm about to give you the steps before the steps. If you already have a process in place and it works for you, continue to use it. If not, the following process might be helpful. To make these steps easier to remember, they all start with the letter *E*. You want to start with the Expectations and continue through to the Experiences.

1. **Expectations.** These are the goals, standards, objectives, or performance descriptors that you want your students to achieve.

2. **Enduring Understandings.** From the expectations, what do you want your students to understand? What are your intentions?

3. **Essential Questions.** Take those understandings and put them in the form of questions such as "Why?" or "How?" These are open-ended questions that offer an inquiry approach to learning.

4. **Evidence.** How will your students show you that they understand?

5. **Evaluation.** Create the assessment that matches the understandings.

6. **Entry Points.** How will you go from the "big" ideas to the smaller ones that will engage your students?

7. **Experiences.** Design your instruction to match your intentions and your assessment, using the seven steps described in this book, to give your students long-term retention and transfer.

Example

Expectation: Students will use a variety of technological and information resources (e.g., libraries, databases, computer networks, video) to gather and synthesize information to create and communicate knowledge.

Enduring Understanding: Knowledge is power.

Essential Question: How can the ability to gather information from various sources make you powerful?

Evidence: Students will demonstrate their ability to gather information through a research report. They will also demonstrate their understanding of various resources through a paper-and-pencil test.

Evaluation: The report will show that the students can evaluate and synthesize information to create and communicate knowledge. The written test will assess their understanding of databases, networks, libraries, and human resources.

Entry Points: Why do you gather information? How is information shared?

Experiences: Using the memory steps for transfer, the students will experience in multiple ways how knowledge is power.

Baby Steps

In essence, you are taking your state or district's expectations and creating the purpose for them. An enduring understanding is the purpose for learning. It is the overarching idea we want our students to internalize about the content area. This understanding is not taught as much as it is discovered through inquiry.

Next, you want to create the questions for inquiry. There are many sources for essential questions. Jan Leonard (2004), an educational consultant dedicated to questioning and inquiry-based learning, has developed a Web site with guiding principles for using this strategy. Leonard offers the following steps to develop essential questions for a unit:

- Identify your unit topic (example: the Civil War).
- Determine the subtopics of the unit (examples: leaders; famous battles; the Underground Railroad; causes and effects).

- Determine the concepts/big ideas that you want your students to walk away with when they're done studying the unit. These can link directly to your state's learning standards. (Example: Illustrate conflicts over the rights and freedom of competing individuals or groups and the impact on future generations.)

- Reword the concepts into questions that begin with words such as *why*, *how*, *should*, *could*, or *which*. (Example: "How did the Civil War impact what goes on in our world today?" or "Which events of the Civil War made the most difference in the result of the war?")

When the essential questions have been formed, you can then decide what the students will need to do to demonstrate their understanding. You will develop the assessment and then determine what experiences will provide the students with the factual and conceptual understandings. When the essential questions can be answered, you will know that the students have the enduring understandings. All of this should come about through the multiple experiences you will provide.

Factors for Learning

Researchers in cognitive neuroscience have found a blend of factors (Arendal & Mann, 2000) that can lead to learning new tasks and concepts successfully:

- **Frequency.** Neural pathways need to build and grow strong by repeated exposure to the learning. In reading, studies have shown that the more a person reads, the better that person will read. Similarly, if you lift weights only occasionally, you will not build up your muscles. But if you lift regularly, you will accomplish your desired fitness level.

- **Intensity.** Learning requires rigorous practice. A student will build neural support for the skill in a shorter period of time if she practices intensely. When my daughter trained for the Chicago Marathon, for example, her workouts were intense in order to prepare her body for the 26.2-mile run.

- **Cross training.** Teaching for memory requires strong networks that can connect to other networks. Therefore, different kinds of skills and different forms of memory should be used.

- **Adaptivity.** Teaching for memory requires that the teacher monitor the student's progress and adjust the teaching/learning situation to meet her needs. In other words, the teacher must differentiate.

- **Motivation and attention.** These factors are what keep students interested in their learning. Various strategies will keep students on task. Frequency and intensity rely on these factors.

The seven steps to teach for memory that I describe in this book incorporate these neuroscience factors as well as the equally important factor of duration. Each step begins with *re-*, the prefix meaning "again" or "back." Memory is a process that takes going over again, and memory is what takes us back in time. As Sir James Matthew Barrie said, "God gave us memories so that we might have roses in December."

Step by Step

The first step, Reach, was going to be Receive, but the latter seemed too unreceptive a word. Our students must be actively involved in their learning. We must reach them, and they must reach out to make gains in their learning. The second step, Reflect, can be defined as "to bring back." We want our students to bring back the information to begin to create an understanding. Step 3, Recode, gives students the opportunity to translate the material and make it their own. Reinforce, step 4, means to "make stronger"; feedback assists the students in knowing where they are in the learning process. Step 5 is Rehearsal, the opportunity to store information more permanently. Examining again describes step 6, Review. The final step is the true test of memory: Retrieve: to recall to mind; to remember. As you ascend the steps, stronger memories are formed, and higher-level thinking takes place (see Figure 1).

Let's take a closer look at each of the steps:

1. Reach. Students are no longer passive in the learning process. Research has shown us that we must engage students in learning. Our classrooms must be student centered rather than teacher centered. Discovery learning, problem-based learning, project-based learning, and inquiry learning have found their place in our

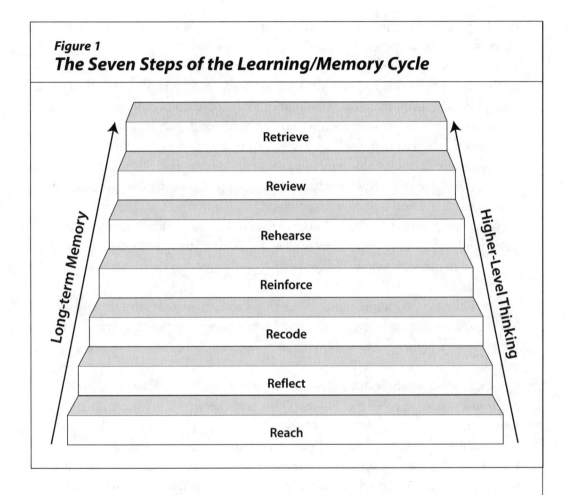

Figure 1
The Seven Steps of the Learning/Memory Cycle

Retrieve

Review

Rehearse

Reinforce

Recode

Reflect

Reach

Long-term Memory

Higher-Level Thinking

schools. In order for any information to be stored in the brain, it must be received through sensory memory. It therefore behooves us to take into consideration attention, motivation, learning styles, emotion, and meaning.

2. Reflect. There's an old joke about teaching being the instructor's ability to take his notes and give a lecture that will go to the student's notes without passing through either's brain. In some cases, I believe that students can take notes robotically and not think at all about the material being presented. Giving students time to "linger over learning" (K. Marshall in Rogers, Ludington, & Graham, 1997), may help make the connections from new material to old. This working memory process can lead to higher-level thinking.

3. Recode. Recoding is a way to organize information in the brain at many levels—an imperative step. Students must take information and make it their own. Using working memory and accessing prior knowledge through long-term memory allow the learner to put information into her own words, pictures, sounds, or movements. Material that is self-generated in this way is better recalled. The recoded material has become a memory and triggers conceptual understanding.

4. Reinforce. From the recoding process, teachers can discover whether student perceptions match their expectations. Through feedback loops, concepts and processes may be perfected. Motivational feedback, informational feedback, or developmental feedback may be desirable. This step offers the teacher the opportunity to catch misconceptions before they become long-term memories that are difficult to change.

5. Rehearse. Both rote rehearsal and elaborative rehearsal have their place in putting information into long-term, permanent memory. Rehearsing in different ways involves higher levels of thinking, including applying, analyzing, and creating.

Strategies for rehearsal and the spacing effect will help teachers and students discover optimal rehearsal techniques. Sleep is also essential in establishing long-term memories.

6. Review. Whereas rehearsal puts information into long-term memory, review presents the opportunity to retrieve that information and manipulate it in working memory. The products of the manipulation can then be returned to long-term memory. As we prepare our students for high-stakes testing, we must match our instruction, review, and assessment to give them the greatest opportunity for achievement. Review must also include test-taking skills.

7. Retrieve. The type of assessment used can affect the student's ability to retrieve stored information. Accessing stored memories may be reliant on specific cues. The retrieval process may also be triggered through recognition techniques as well as recall. Stress can inhibit the ability to access memories and must also be addressed.

The following chapters describe how to develop these steps, how to access higher levels of thinking, and how these relate to brain activity and brain research. Step-by-step we can teach the way the brain learns, take advantage of research-based strategies, and ensure that our students have the ability to transfer information in new and unanticipated circumstances. We *can* teach for memory!

Reflection Section

Keeping in mind that the reflection process should be encouraged after each step, I end each chapter itself with a reflection section. If you have not already reflected about what you have read, take this opportunity to do so. As you were reading, questions may have come to mind. Think about those questions: Where will you find the answers, and how do they relate to your present situation? If you were taking notes or highlighting, go back over those areas and think about why they may be important to you. Need more information now? Check the reference section for further reading, or read on!

Reach

If you can't reach them, you can't teach them.

For most of us, our favorite teacher was someone we felt really cared about and/or challenged us: someone who recognized us and reached out to us.

—*Jonathan Cohen*, Educating Minds and Hearts

I am facing another difficult class of 29 8th graders. They are from a variety of back-grounds. Four of them have been expelled from other schools. Two of them have older brothers who are involved in gang activity. Seventeen come from single-parent homes. Several of them are on welfare. One has a father in prison.

The first day I have to go over the rules in the handbook. Those who are following along are laughing and making snide remarks—too softly for me to hear exactly what they say. I pass out books and collect emergency cards, and finally the day is over.

The second day I decide to take the students for a "book walk" through the social studies text. I have read recently that pre-exposure to the material will help students feel more comfortable later when we cover it. Two students start a verbal battle over some of the content. Fifteen others join in. My room is next to the principal's office, and I fear the ruckus is being overheard. My heart is racing. I look at the clock, praying it is time for the bell. No such luck. I wonder why teachers on television and in movies are "saved by the bell" and I am not. I open my desk drawer and pull out a whistle. One quick blow and they quiet down. Surprised. Some angry. But quiet. I give them a quick assignment—they are to draw a picture of any historical event they want. I sit and wait for the class to end.

The bell rings and I beat the students out the door. I run into—almost literally—one of my colleagues. I look him in the eye and say, "I cannot teach these kids!"

He looks back at me and with total seriousness says, "Sure you can, but first, you have to get their attention. If you can't do that, you can get a different job."

I was taken aback by his comments. But I knew he was right. I have had a lot of teaching experience at all levels. I started thinking about how I was able to reach those other classes. I knew the whistle only worked because it was novel. Should I come up with other novel ideas? What else might be valuable? To reach my students I would need their attention. I would also need emotional connections and good working relationships with my students. I would need to understand their learning styles, and I would need to make the material relevant to their lives.

We are bombarded with sensory stimuli throughout the day. According to neuroscientist Michael Gazzaniga (1999), our brain retains only about one percent of that information. How do we help our students hold onto even the sensory information, let alone all the semantic information they need to remember? According to Shaun Kerry (2002), of the American Board of Psychiatry and Neurology, whether certain events or information are retained in memory is "dependent upon an individual's love for the subject matter and its dramatic, emotional, auditory, and visual impact."

Many factors affect our students' ability to secure information. But my colleague said I first have to get their attention.

What Is Attention?

It is time for Writer's Workshop. The 3rd graders are scattered throughout the room. There is a low buzz of conversation as some of the students discuss their writing with others. The teacher is conferencing with J.D.

Seated quietly at her desk is Katie. She is rereading her short essay on her favorite book. As she reads, she pauses to draw a picture depicting an episode in the book. Jamie approaches Katie's desk and asks to borrow a blue marker. Katie stops reading and hands the marker to her. Jamie glances at the picture Katie is making and asks her several questions about the book. Katie colors in the house she has drawn as she describes the characters and the scene. Interrupting the conversation, Angelo says he needs to get a book out of the desk Katie is seated in. He excuses himself and starts looking for the book. Katie must stand now to color while she carries on her account to Jamie.

With her right hand, Katie maintains her coloring, and with her left hand she grabs the book she has spotted for Angelo. He thanks her and goes back to his place at the table where the students are peer editing. Jamie's interest is piqued and she asks for the name of the author of Katie's book. Katie has loaned the book to Tiffany, who sits across the aisle. The girls ask Tiffany who the author is and maintain their dialogue as they await a response. Katie is listening to Jamie's comment about the book as she admires her picture. She is also listening for Tiffany's voice to tell her the author's name. Katie picks up a green marker and draws a large tree next to the house as Tiffany reads the author's name and Jamie returns to her seat.

According to Andreason (2001), *attention* is the cognitive process that allows Katie to control irrelevant stimuli (ignore the buzz of conversation in the room), to notice important stimuli (her essay, her picture, and Jamie's comments), and to shift from one stimulus to another (from talking to Jamie to drawing the picture, and from interacting with Angelo to interacting with Jamie and Tiffany). She was balancing visual information in the picture. She attended to auditory information as she listened to Jamie and for Tiffany. The tactile information she was dealing with included drawing her picture, grabbing the book for Angelo, and giving Jamie the marker.

Andreason (2001) divides attention into five types: sustained, directed, selective, divided, and focused. *Sustained* attention involves focusing for a long period of time. Creating lesson plans or creating an assessment requires this type of attention. *Directed* attention occurs when we consciously select a particular stimulus from all that bombards us. This is the attention we give one particular student if she is disrupting the class. *Selective* attention involves focusing on one particular stimulus for a personal or sensible reason. For instance, a student may select to listen to a whisper from another student rather than to the lecture being given.

Divided attention occurs as we rapidly shift focus from one thing to another. Our students are dealing with divided attention as they do their homework in front of the television. *Focused* attention is directing attention to a particular aspect of some stimulus, such as asking our students to focus on the answer to an essential question as they research on the Internet.

Attention is necessary for thinking. The brain scans the environment, sifting through sensory messages to find something to pay attention to. The brain is always attending; our students just may not be attending to what we desire. Attention requires three elements: arousal, orientation, and focus (Carter, 1998).

The reticular activating system (see Appendix A) controls arousal levels through the amount of neurotransmitter it emits. Stimulation of the frontal lobes by norepinephrine and dopamine changes the brain's electrical activity and causes us to be alert. At this time, the parietal lobe disengages from the current stimulus, and we are oriented to the new stimulus. The thalamus then controls the situation and allows us to focus as it carries the new information to the frontal lobes. The thalamus has the power to inhibit other sensory stimulation to aid us. The anterior cingulate allows us to maintain attention (Carter, 1998). The hippocampus is a major player in the attention process. Because of its access to so many memories, if the reticular activating system reacts to some sensory stimulation, the hippocampus can compare it to old experiences and determine its novelty (Ratey, 2001).

This biological information is helpful for educators. It tells us that the attention process can be aided by instruction. In other words, the anterior cingulate will focus on what we bring its attention to.

Noah is playing on his computer. It is seven o'clock, but he is too engrossed in his game to realize that time is passing quickly. His computer suddenly freezes, and he has to reboot. While waiting for the machine to come back online, Noah glances at the clock. He can't believe time slipped by so fast.

Noah's reticular activating system aroused him. He has a load of homework to complete and obviously didn't realize how time flies!

Noah looks at his stack of books. He begins to prioritize. "Let's see. I might be able to get my English done on the bus tomorrow. I have to finish my math now because I may need Mom's help. Then I'd better practice those words for my spelling test."

It's Noah's frontal lobes that are now orienting him to his homework. They are helping him plan and prioritize.

Noah pulls his math book from the pile, opens his notebook, and is completely focused on his work. He doesn't hear his mom open the door to look in on him.

Noah's thalamus has filtered out sensory stimuli that will not aid him in his current focus of attention, his math homework.

Mental Note: Without awareness of incoming information, explicit learning cannot occur.

What About Motivation?

Jeremy and Joe are good friends. They've attended school together since kindergarten. Their mothers belong to the same book club, and their fathers often golf together.

On this sunny Saturday afternoon, Jeremy and Joe are going to the batting cages. Baseball season is right around the corner, and they're hoping to move from the junior varsity team to varsity. They are just gathering their bats when Joe's dad approaches.

"Hey, guys, how about coming to the course with us this afternoon? We could use some good caddies," he asks.

Jeremy's face immediately lights up. "That sounds like fun. I could use some pointers on my golf game, and it's really a great day to be out in the sunshine! Don't you think so, Joe? We can go to the cages afterward. You've been saying you want to try out for the golf team. This could be a great opportunity."

Joe, however, is not convinced. When his dad looks at him for a reply and sees the negative look on his face, he sighs and says, "OK, Joe, we'll pay you for your trouble."

Joe nods his head. "OK, but it has to be more than 10 bucks. That's what you gave me last time—I won't do it for that."

Two similar boys with similar interests, yet their responses are quite different. Of course, many factors may be involved in this scenario, but the bottom line is that Joe required an *extrinsic* motivation, while Jeremy was happy to caddy for *intrinsic* reasons.

Why We Do the Things We Do

Merriam-Webster (1993) defines *motive* as "something (as a need or desire) that causes a person to act" (p. 759). Asking my students about their needs resulted in a very long list. Interestingly enough, none of the content that I teach ever showed up on their lists. In other words, students do not see reading, math, history, science, or writing as a necessity! To motivate our students, we have to prove to them that our topics are necessary, or we must make them desirable.

Jeremy and Joe were each motivated in different ways. *Intrinsic* motivation comes from within—a desire or need that the brain determines is pleasurable or important. When we are intrinsically motivated, neurotransmitters such as dopamine are released in our brains (LeDoux, 2002). This provides the "get up and go" that is necessary to accomplish our goal. These same neurotransmitters are released when our goal is attained. Dopamine, the pleasure chemical, makes us want to achieve again to repeat the good feeling.

Extrinsic motivation is associated with rewards and punishment. Some researchers, such as Alfie Kohn (1993), believe that extrinsic motivators change the brain and shift the goal from attaining the objective to attaining some tangible reward or avoiding a punishment. The concern is that receiving the reward will cause dopamine to be released and this will train the brain to have good feelings about the reward as opposed to the accomplishment.

In our sample scenario, Jeremy is seeking his dopamine from the experience and the learning, whereas Joe seeks his from the payment. Many researchers believe that the external reward must get larger to receive the same level of pleasure or excitement. So the $10 doesn't make Joe as happy as it used to, and he demands more.

    Mental Note: Students are motivated in different ways.

Maslow's Hierarchy

According to Abraham Maslow's theory, certain needs must be met before the brain can focus on academic achievement. His hierarchy begins with physiological needs and then proceeds to safety, belonging, esteem, and, finally, self-actualization (Maslow & Lowery, 1998).

Physiological needs. These consist of basic survival requirements. Food, water, shelter, and clothing fall into this category. If a student is hungry, that hunger will remain the number one priority until it is satisfied. Attention will always be focused on unmet needs.

Safety needs. Security, freedom from threat, and predictability are all-important to the brain's need for safety. If the physiological needs are met, the brain focuses on the safety needs. Once these are met, it turns itself toward the next level. If our students feel safe and unthreatened in our classrooms, their levels of focus and attention are not impeded.

Belonging and love. These two needs comprise a primary motivator for the brain. People seek to overcome loneliness when their physical needs have been met and they feel safe. Relationships with friends, spouses, and children provide a sense of belonging. Students who have good relationships with their teacher and other students have neurotransmitters such as serotonin and dopamine released in their brains to make them feel good and feel motivated.

Esteem needs. Self-respect, achievement and success, and a good reputation fall into this category. Feeling valuable in the classroom helps our students focus. Especially when they feel valuable to the teacher, they put forth more effort.

Self-actualization. This level is defined as becoming what the individual is most suited for. Attaining this highest level on the hierarchy is an incredible accomplishment that we want for all of our students. They must first know that they are safe, that they belong and are valued, and that they can respect themselves as others respect them.

To reach our students, we must be aware of these needs. Every effort must be made to meet the needs of our students so they will be able to attend to the information we want them to learn and remember.

Glasser's Choice Theory of Motivation

William Glasser (1999) defines five equally important needs: survival, belonging and love, power, freedom, and fun. On the cover of his popular book *Choice Theory* is a statement that epitomizes this theory: "Choosing the life you want and staying close to the people you need."

From his theory, we can conclude that offering choices to our students (responding to their needs for power and freedom) may also make them feel good about what they are doing and therefore make them more motivated and attentive. Belonging and love encompass the latter part of the statement. Students need to feel close to others and know that they can rely on their teacher and their peers.

According to Brophy (1987), student motivation is an acquired competence developed "through general experience, but it is stimulated through modeling, communication of expectations, and direct instruction or socialization by significant others" (p. 41). Therefore, the classroom environment—how the teacher affects the socialization process, what the expectations are and how they are communicated, and the modeling component—can significantly influence student motivation and attention.

Mental Note: The brain cannot focus on learning if basic needs are not met.

How Emotions Affect Learning

Vanessa is in the school storeroom gathering material for an art project. Art is not her favorite subject, and her selection shows little effort toward creativity. She has collected markers, paper, and rulers. Nothing is sparking ideas for the assignment called "My Ideal Spot." Vanessa doesn't want to spend a lot of time on this project because she has two other assignments to complete. As she wanders up one aisle and down another, she spots Jessie. Jessie is a student who does it all. She takes ballet and piano, writes award-winning essays, and is very artistic. She loves projects like this. Jessie is bright and lets others know it.

Vanessa notices Jessie's acquisitions. She has filled her arms with glue, glitter, cotton, clay, and oil paint. Vanessa turns to avoid Jessie, who will undoubtedly brag about her project, but it's too late. Jessie walks up to Vanessa and looks at her meager collection of items. She smiles and pushes her heavy load toward Vanessa. She glances down at the markers and asks, "You just getting started?"

Vanessa feels totally inadequate and replies, "Yes, I just got here and grabbed some of the usuals. Now I'm backtracking to get the good stuff."

"So, what's your project going to be?" Jessie queries. Vanessa suspects that she is just asking so she can outdo her with a fabulous project idea.

Vanessa tries to think quickly and responds with, "Oh, my ideal spot is a secret place that I share with my friends. I have to check with them and make sure it's OK to use it for this project." Vanessa thought that should quiet her down. After all, Jessie probably doesn't have a spot she shares with friends!

"Well, my ideal spot is in Hawaii. My family goes there every year for two weeks. There are wonderful beaches and an awesome volcano. When I told the art teacher about my idea, he was so excited to see it." Jessie rambles on mentioning plants and places that Vanessa has never heard of. Her mind wanders until she picks up on Jessie's last comment: "Vanessa, if you ever want to learn how to create a fabulous project, let me know."

Vanessa is overcome with anger and embarrassment. She opens her mouth to give Jessie a witty reply, but nothing comes out! Her brain just can't seem to grasp any smart-aleck remarks. She smiles at her with clenched teeth and walks away.

Vanessa is seething. How dare Jessie make a remark like that? "I can do my own art project," she thinks. "I certainly don't need her help. I should have just let her have it, but I'm too much of a lady for that. Why couldn't I think of a comeback? I'm the comeback queen. I always have a comment for everyone."

Vanessa's emotions had her tongue-tied. Goleman (1995) calls this an emotional "hijacking." Higher-level thinking doesn't take place when this phenomenon occurs. Vanessa was stuck in the emotional center of her brain and couldn't access the creative center. A few hours later she had several responses for Jessie. She almost called her to share them!

Emotions have a strong influence on learning (Small, 2002). If students are anxious, depressed, or even angry, they do not receive information in an efficient way. The brain is captivated by the emotion and turns attention to it. When these emotions capture the brain's attention, working memory is flooded and cannot be effective in working with the task at hand.

That's one way that emotions affect learning. There is, however, a very positive side to emotion.

Mental Note: Strong emotions can impede the reception of information.

Reaching Students Through Their Emotions

What are emotions? Most researchers refer to the six universal emotions: happiness, sadness, fear, anger, surprise, and disgust. These are primary emotions that are found and recognized in all humans all over the world. Secondary emotions are socially oriented; jealousy, guilt, and embarrassment are a few. Finally, some emotions are what Damasio (1999) calls "background emotions" which include tension and well-being.

Emotions are produced at subcortical regions of the brain; they are part of a set of structures that represent body states. Involuntarily engaged, without conscious knowledge, they affect both the brain and the body. Emotions and emotional states are patterns of response that lead to behavior. This emotion and behavior can occur when someone perceives information through the senses or when an individual conjures up certain memories (Damasio, 1999). The emotions Vanessa was having when encountering Jessica represent sensory information. Those same emotions can be rekindled when she thinks of the situation later on. When Vanessa next runs into Jessica, those emotions may resurface and affect her behavior.

The amygdala is the major player in emotions and their memories. Because the amygdala modulates both explicit and implicit memory due to its location and access to incoming information, we remember poignant events better than boring or neutral ones (Bloom, Beal, & Kupfer, 2003).

According to LeDoux (2002), "Attention, perception, memory, decision-making, and the conscious concomitants of each are all swayed in emotional states . . . emotional arousal organizes and coordinates brain activity" (p. 225). Schacter (2001), in *The Seven Sins of Memory*, states, "Everyday experience and laboratory studies reveal that emotionally charged incidents are better remembered than non-emotional events. The emotional boost begins at the moment that a memory is born, when attention and elaboration strongly influence whether an experience will be subsequently remembered or forgotten" (p. 163).

Stephen Hamann of Emory University uses magnetic resonance imaging (MRI) to gauge emotional responses to words and pictures (Hamann, Ely, Grafton, & Kilts, 1999). The imaging shows the activation of the amygdala when individuals respond to an emotional sight. "When the amygdala detects emotion, it essentially boosts activity in areas of the brain that form memories," says Hamann. "And that's how it makes a stronger memory and a more vivid memory" (p. 292). Subjects in Hamann's experiments remember twice as many emotional words as neutral ones.

Because emotions are so powerful, incorporating emotion into our teaching is an excellent way to reach our students. If emotion organizes brain activity, and attention and perception are swayed by emotional states, then our everyday experiences in school will become more memorable if we use emotions to reach our students.

Remember, we are just at the first step: reaching our students. If we want to teach for memory, we must start with the basics: What will engage our students' brains? What will they attend to? The brain is always attending to something, and we want to be the first priority.

Emotional Hooks

You are the expert in your classroom with your students. Here are some possible ways to pull your students emotionally into your lessons. Make your presentation exciting. Excitatory neurotransmitters are released when we feel excited. Norepinephrine starts a cascade of chemical responses that increase the intensity of the experience and the perception of it.

- Emotions are contagious (Lewis, Amini, & Lannon, 2000), so act excited yourself. What is exciting about what you are going to teach them?

- Dress in a costume that will get their admiration or even their disapproval. Know that it will at least get their attention!

- Play music that fits the theme of what you are teaching. Music has emotional anchors for many.

- Begin the lesson with a story. It can be a personal story that you somehow relate to the topic at hand, or it can be a secondhand story with connections to the topic. The brain loves stories, as it is a natural way for the brain to organize information (Caine & Caine, 1994).

- Begin the class by asking students to make a choice. If the issue you will be studying has two sides, divide the room in half, and have students choose a side as they enter. Put up two posters, one on each side of the room, to indicate what each side believes.

Mental Note: Emotions take precedence over all other brain processes.

Use Advance Organizers to Focus Attention

"We often see what we expect to see" (Marzano, Pickering, Norford, et al., 2001, p. 279). Advance organizers are powerful instruments for focusing our students' attention. These organizers come in many packages. For instance, an advance organizer could be an oral presentation of the subject matter and how it relates to prior knowledge. In my experience, the most effective tool was a graphic organizer that focused my students and directed them to the learning I intended them to remember. Graphic organizers provide a framework for the learning, and they keep the students within that structure.

My favorite organizer is the agree/disagree chart (Burke, 1999; see Figure 1.1). Such a chart is composed of statements that can be presented orally or in writing. I prefer a chart with statements on them and a place to check "agree" or "disagree."

Figure 1.1
Agree/Disagree Chart

	Agree	Disagree
1. Younger people remember more than older people.		
2. Age has nothing to do with memory.		
3. Memory is stored in one area of the brain.		
4. You only have enough immediate memory space for a phone number.		
5. Females have better memories than males.		
6. You never forget how to ride a bike.		
7. It is easier to forget than to remember.		
8. Smells trigger certain memories.		

The agree/disagree statements will evoke emotions in most students. They also help them understand the concepts that are being shared.

Advance organizers call on prior knowledge. If the students have no previous experience with the subject, you can ask them to make an attempt to agree or disagree. When the unit is nearly finished, I give my students another opportunity to read the statements and agree or disagree. They then compare the original chart with the recent one. Some students are amazed at what they have learned, while others pat themselves on the back for what they already knew.

Most graphic organizers can be used as advance organizers (see Appendix B for several examples). Again, they may help you reach the students as they provide a scaffold for the learning. Some other graphic organizers that may be helpful include the following:

- Venn diagrams help students see similarities and differences.

- Mind mapping is a helpful way to organize new material. Recent research has shown it is especially helpful for dyslexic students.

- KWHLU charts help students pay attention. *K* is for what you already know, *W* for what you want to know, *H* for how you want to learn it, *L* for what you have learned, and *U* for how you will use it in your world.

- Hierarchy diagrams may be useful for classification purposes.

- A T chart, or two-column chart, can be used to organize many content areas.

- Sequencing charts are great for stories or history time frames.

Mental Note: Show the brain what to focus on.

Connecting with Students Through Learning Styles

Our students have different ways of learning. Some of them are visual learners, some auditory, and some kinesthetic or tactile. These learning preferences or learning strengths may influence what our students are paying special attention to (Sprenger, 2003).

Visual learners. These learners are probably thrilled with graphic organizers, overhead transparencies, and perhaps even the textbook. They may have an easier time "getting the picture" if you are a visual teacher. They will pay particular attention to visual information, including text. School is usually accommodating to these learners. To reach them for attention purposes, brightly colored pictures, video clips, and handouts may grab them.

Auditory learners. These students need to talk as much as they like to listen. Information becomes real to them through discussion. Your pictures, overheads, and handouts may be lost on these learners, but they love to jump into a discussion. To reach these students initially, music or debate may be a key. Their memories are strongly auditory in nature; in other words, they remember what they hear over what they see or feel.

Kinesthetic and tactile learners. They may wiggle and jiggle or need hands-on learning. For these students, movement is inevitable, so controlled movement is always preferred. They may need to "become" what they are learning about. To engage their attention, an activity that allows them to role-play, create a concept, or work with technology such as a computer may be helpful.

Consider the following:

The freshmen students enter the classroom. It is a warm, almost oppressive day. The windows are open, but little air is circulating.

It is time to begin a unit on the Civil War. This is not a favorite of mine. Perhaps it is because my own history teacher did a mediocre job of presenting it. With this heat, I am not in the mood to teach at all, let alone approach a challenging topic.

"OK, kids," I begin, "I know you're hot. I am, too. This may be tough, but it's time we started studying the Civil War. Does anyone know anything about that war?"

Now, I could have begun this way:

Music is playing in the background. I have chosen "I Wish I Was in Dixie." The students look at me a little strangely. I hand them cups of water as they enter the room, and as the final bell rings, I turn the music off and say, "Walk around the room and look at the Civil War posters and paraphernalia. As warm as we are today, I want you to realize that the soldiers who fought in this war were wearing heavy uniforms and were out in the sun continuously.

"How many of you have seen Gone with the Wind? *It's a great movie; of course, Rhett Butler makes it even more interesting. Do you remember that there was a lot of bloodshed? I hope that blood doesn't bother you all. It really was a bloody war!"*

The second scenario is more of an attention getter for several reasons. First, some emotions were evoked with the mention of blood and Rhett Butler, and the use of music. Second, I used a multisensory approach. As soon as the students entered, they began moving, listening, and looking. Finally, I related their present experience of being hot and uncomfortable to the individuals we were about to study. I gave them water to fulfill a physiological need as well as to let them know that I understand how they are feeling, that we are in this together.

> **Mental Note: Students with a strong learning style preference will be reached most easily through that style.**

Relationships

The feeling of togetherness that I was able to convey to my students is only accessible if I have taken the time to set up relationships with each of them. This is the key to learning in any situation and with people of any age. Our relationships offer the framework in which we understand our progress and appreciate the usefulness of what we're learning (Goleman, Boyatzis, & McKee, 2002).

Four emotional intelligence domains can be applied to relationship building in any environment: self-awareness, self-management, social awareness, and relationship management. The first two deal with personal skills; the last two are related to social skills.

Personal skills. Recognizing one's own emotions is critical to attaining the other competencies. If our students know how they feel, they are then able, with guidance, to learn how to manage those emotions. We hope that our students come to school with these abilities, but sometimes it behooves us to add these to our repertoire, as it will make teaching and learning much easier.

Social skills. A primary skill in this domain is empathy. The ability to sense others' emotions, understand their perspectives, and show concern can foster powerful teacher–student and student–student relationships in the classroom. Relationship management includes managing conflict, influencing others, and cultivating relationships.

The passions that any of us have to do our work may come from pure emotion like excitement, from the satisfaction that we get from the learning, or from the joy of working with others. Any of these motivators activate the left prefrontal cortex, which receives many of those "feel good" neurotransmitters. Simultaneously, the prefrontal circuits quiet feelings of frustration that might interfere with the learning (Goleman et al., 2002).

Finding Connections to Each Other

Building relationships with students requires finding common ground. The more they feel they are like you or like each other, the more comfortable it is to develop relationships that will enhance learning. One method I like to use I borrowed from a 5th grade teacher. It's a get-to-know-each-other activity with a twist (see Figure 1.2). Students receive a sheet divided into boxes to be signed by classmates who

Figure 1.2
Get-to-Know-Each-Other Activity

Find someone who . . .

Has a dog	Has brown eyes	Likes Pepsi more than Coke
Watches *Friends*	Reads a lot	Loves chocolate chip cookies
Has red as a favorite color	Listens to books on tape	Thinks M&M's are good chocolate
Plays chess	Likes computers	Prefers gold rather than silver
Has a red car	Has two sisters	Is afraid of heights
Travels a lot	Enjoys music	Likes to run
Plays golf	Plays checkers	Has a brother

meet the criteria stated in each square. Students walk around asking others if they like chocolate chip cookies, for example, or have a red car. The rules are that they cannot shove the sheet in the other student's face and say, "Here—sign one." They must approach a fellow student and ask a question pertaining to the sheet. After the sheet is completed, everyone sits down. I then go through each category and ask the students to raise their hands if the category pertains to them. They can look around and see what they have in common with others in the room. The sheets I first use are characteristics that are true of me. The students quickly see what we have in common. A second sheet is given a few weeks later after I have had the opportunity to get personal information from them via index cards. This time the students see how many other students have things in common with them or share their special interests.

Social Categories and Empathy

According to Giannetti and Sagarese's (2001) research in their book *Cliques*, our students fall into one of four social categories. The most obvious is perhaps the *Popular* group, made up of students who may be attractive, athletic, and affluent. Setting the stage for what is "in," these students comprise about 35 percent of the student population. The emotional issue with this particular group is that popularity isn't necessarily permanent. These kids may be worrying about how to keep their social status.

Another category, making up about 10 percent of the population, is the *Fringe* group. These students sometimes get to hang out with the Popular group but often are left behind. This social position seems to please them enough to put up with the times they are not included. As a result, these kids are never sure whether they are popular. Modeling themselves after the Popular group, but not knowing exactly where they belong, is an emotional issue for them.

The third category is called *Friendship Circles*. These are small groups of students who are good friends. They realize they are not popular, but they have each other and appear to be content. These groups make up about 45 percent of the population, and circle members seem to feel pretty good about themselves.

Finally, we have the *Loners*. The 10 percent of the kids who have few or no friends at all make up this cluster. The Loners may be bright, ambitious, and light-years ahead of their peers, or they may have poor social skills and be difficult to be around. Although these students would possibly like to be a part of a group, they are simply not accepted. Sometimes these kids may be bitter about their social situation and may even lash out.

According to this research, only 45 percent of our students feel confident in their social/emotional position in school. After such school tragedies as the Columbine experience, it behooves us to become attentive to the social structure in our school. One place to discover cliques is to visit the cafeteria at lunchtime. A social stratum plays itself out as students discover who they may or may not eat with. To set up strong relationships, all of these students must be able to interact with each other and respect each difference and gift. Empathy plays a large part in this ability.

My 9-year-old Sheltie is very ill, and I have to have her put to sleep by the vet. I arrange to take her and stay for the procedure early one morning while my first hour class is in the library. After the emotional ordeal, I return to school. I stop by the office and tell the administrators that I have indeed returned. My eyes are red from crying, but I know I can manage my emotions in my classroom.

One of my colleagues expresses her sympathy and then as a reminder says, "Don't let those kids see you cry!"

I nod and walk despondently down the hall. When I reach the library door, I feel an enormous sadness and some anger at what my coworker had said. Can't I express my emotions? Wouldn't my students think that I am heartless if I weren't upset? And isn't this an excellent opportunity to teach empathy?

I enter the room and all eyes are on me.

"You're here!" says one of the girls.

"Are you sick?" another asks.

"No," I reply. "I just had a very sad experience." I explain the reason for my tardiness.

"My cat had to be put to sleep, Mrs. Sprenger," Nancy offers. "I felt really bad."

"I'm sure you did," I acknowledge.

"It's just a dumb animal," Brett announces.

I look at Brett, and the students look at me. "Have you ever had a pet?" I ask.

"Yeah, we got a dog. He sleeps in my room," Brett shares.

The students begin to dialogue about loss. Brett sits quietly until the conversation ends with the bell. He walks over to me on his way out the door. "I'm sorry, Mrs. S., I guess I didn't really think about how it would feel. I'd be upset, just like you."

Two lessons were begun that day. First, the students were able to put them-selves in my shoes and understand how I was feeling. Second, they recognized my feelings and saw that I could manage them. According to Comer (2003), "children need to form emotional bonds with their teachers and see healthy social relation-ships among the adults in their lives to function well in school" (p. 11).

> **Mental Note: Attention and motivation can be directed through personal relationships with students.**

"Why Do I Have to Know This Stuff?"

How many times have we heard this question? When we think about relevance, we can again look at the brain and how it learns and remembers. The brain is pattern seeking. It takes new information and searches long-term memory to find a pattern to "hook" it to. If you look at Figure 1.3, your brain sees a square. Is it really there?

Figure 1.3
Searching for a Familiar Pattern

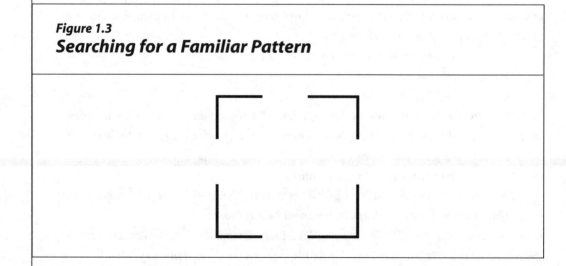

No, but you have a pattern in your brain for squares, and this is what your brain finds to connect the image to. It fills in the blanks (Jensen, 2001).

When we offer information to our students, their brains try to make some connections to patterns already stored. If there are no connections, the information is easily dropped. Relevancy involves making some associations that affect their lives.

This is not a simple task when we look at the standards and benchmarks that we must reach. Research shows that students perform better when they are provided with criteria, models, and examples that clearly illustrate our expectations (Schmoker, 1999).

A student-centered classroom can be created with project-based learning and inquiry learning as well. These learning activities focus on information-processing skills and lead to understanding. Reaching our students through relevant issues increases the chances that information will enter the memory process.

Which of the following scenarios do you believe would be more appealing to your students?

Scenario 1

Miss Owen's students enter the classroom. They immediately take their seats and get out their notebooks. Today they are studying the Lewis and Clark expedition. They know this because Miss Owen has it written on the overhead.

As soon as the bell rings, Miss Owen begins disseminating information verbally (i.e., lecturing). Some students frantically take notes. Others lose their focus quickly and gaze around the room. Miss Owen has some posters up depicting the events of the expedition. Perhaps some of her students will learn something from the posters.

Scenario 2

Miss Owen's students enter the classroom. On the overhead is a picture of a huge mosquito. Beneath the picture is written, "You are part of the Lewis and Clark expedition. One of the biggest nuisances you have are the mosquitoes. They are everywhere. There are times when it is difficult to breathe without inhaling a bug! Research ways that your expedition can deal with this situation. Compare your information with what we would do today."

Posters, books, and Internet access are available to the students. They are divided into groups and begin their work.

Miss Owen's students in the second scenario learned much more than how to handle mosquitoes. Approaching this part of history with a problem that all could relate to was an invitation to learn. Her students followed the entire expedition as they followed those insects.

She also brought relevancy by having her students create a Venn diagram comparing what Lewis and Clark took with them on this trip and what their families would pack (Figure 1.4).

Making content relevant to our students' lives allows them to start making connections to prior knowledge immediately. Problem-based learning is experiential learning that is built around a real-world problem. Students engage in the

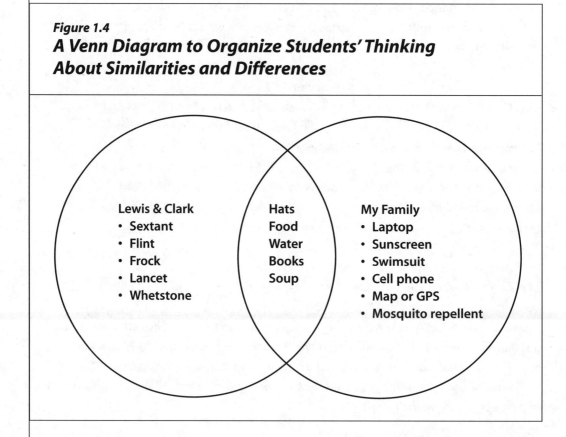

Figure 1.4
A Venn Diagram to Organize Students' Thinking About Similarities and Differences

Lewis & Clark
- Sextant
- Flint
- Frock
- Lancet
- Whetstone

Hats
Food
Water
Books
Soup

My Family
- Laptop
- Sunscreen
- Swimsuit
- Cell phone
- Map or GPS
- Mosquito repellent

process of identifying the problem and then finding a solution. This is an open-ended approach to learning the standards. These problems should approximate what a professional in the field would tackle in the real world (Wiggins & McTighe, 1998).

Relevancy, Relationships, and the Real World

Many of our diverse learners have difficulty relating to our goals and standards. Students from extreme povery may be focusing on survival. Reading with fluency, understanding different forms of government, and knowing and applying concepts that explain how living things function, adapt, and change may not be the most crucial things to them. Nevertheless, it is our job to help students reach those benchmarks. The most powerful thing we can do is to help them find the relationship between their lives and our goals. It's not an easy task.

Here is an example using an Illinois State Learning Goal in Social Science:

STATE GOALS 15: Understand economic systems, with an emphasis on the U.S.

Benchmark 15 B. Understand that scarcity necessitates choices by consumers.

Essential question relevant to students: If you have limited resources for entertainment, how do you make your choices?

Source: www.isbe.net/ils/socscience/sog15.html.

I would put an example like this up on the board so the students would see what the goal is behind the instruction. When the question "Why do we have to know this stuff?" would come up, I would simply point to the board.

We must always deal with contextualization—that is, how our students know about and understand our concepts. Let them tell their stories. Those stories hold prior knowledge, provide other students with hooks to the new information, and hold their attention. By allowing students to share their stories, you are building relationships in the classroom among students and between you and the storyteller. If there is little relevancy to what you are teaching, it may be the relationship you have with the students that keeps them motivated.

Mental Note: Our students remember what affects their lives.

A Novel Approach

Teachers have their own ways of reaching students, and often instinctively they know when it's time to try something new. Novelty is appealing to the brain. Perhaps you remember how the reticular activating system filters information. When anything is perceived as unusual, it releases norepinephrine to wake up the brain. Once something has been repeated, the brain habituates to it, and the novelty is gone (Ratey, 2001). Here are a few ideas to add novelty to your instruction:

- Begin with a bizarre fact that relates to your content. (Did you know that Abraham Lincoln wore bow ties?)
- Accessorize. (Wear a bow tie.)
- Hang something from the light or the overhead. (A bowtie?)
- Use a whistle or other sound your students are not accustomed to hearing.
- Play music pertaining to your content.
- Use a PowerPoint presentation with animation.

From Sensory to Immediate Memory

We know through cognitive research that attention, motivation, relationships, relevance, learning styles, and emotions are essential components of the "reaching" process. If we can get information from sensory memory into immediate memory, then we are on our way to long-term retention. As people mentally prepare for a task, they activate the prefrontal cortex, the area that performs higher-level functions and puts them in action. This advance preparation ensures that they will perform better than without prior activation (Carter et al., 2000).

Reflection

1. Be aware of possible distractions in your classroom. For instance, auditory learners may be sensitive to sounds. If you can't have that noisy radiator fixed, try to seat the sound-sensitive student as far from the distraction as possible.

2. Think about extrinsic motivators that you may be using now. Some may be appropriate and necessary, but are others possibly undermining your students' innate desire to learn?

3. Discuss with colleagues ways to make your content more meaningful to your students. How can you explain the necessity of the content? Or can you make it more desirable? Can you create interdisciplinary units that would be more relevant to your students?

4. Examine the climate of your classroom. Are you meeting the needs of your students? Are they comfortable with you and their peers? Could you change anything to make things better?

Reflect

Reflection is not a luxury; it is a necessity.

Thinking and talking about experiences not only helps to make sense of
the past, but also changes the likelihood of subsequent remembering.

—*Daniel Schacter*, The Seven Sins of Memory

"This is a waste of my time!"

*I look up from my desk, quite surprised to realize that the voice is that of one
of my successful students. It is Patti, a good student who usually performs well
enough for a B. I believe she could earn As, but there seems to be a tiny disconnect
between her receiving and retrieving systems. She almost always has that "aha"
moment. I can see it in her face, and she is sometimes verbal about her feelings, as
she is today.*

*"I only asked you to take a few minutes and write what you've learned and
what you can do with it," I offer.*

*She looks at me, frustrated. "Yeah, but, Mrs. Sprenger, I'm just getting into this
unit, and I don't want to stop and think about this junk."*

*"Patti, trust me. I really believe that this task will make a difference in how
well you remember what you're learning," I respond.*

"So, we're supposed to stop our group discussions, get out our journals, and write a 'So What? Now What?' page. That's going to help? I didn't think I'd like to study anything about alternate forms of energy, and I'm enjoying it. This is like being interrupted in the middle of a TV show!"

At this point, several students have stopped writing and are nodding at her words. One speaks up.

"Patti's right. Aren't we wasting time?" he asks.

"Listen. I'm trying this strategy because a professor of mine made me do it in a graduate class. It really helped my memory, and I think this type of strategy may add to what you remember. I believe it's worth a try, so do it, please," I request. I return to my own journal.

This changes the tone of my own reflection. I write "So What? Now What?" and reflect, "Maybe this wasn't a good idea. It really works for me, but maybe not for kids. Or am I just letting them instill doubts? The research says the brain needs time to reflect. I hope this works!"

A few weeks later, Patti enters my room sheepishly.

"Mrs. Sprenger? Look at this," she says. She hands me a graded test, not from my class but from her math class. The paper has an A written across the top. The teacher has commented, "Patti, this is your best work. Your extended response answer shows that you have put some thought into your problem solving. Keep up the good work!"

"Congratulations!" I respond.

"Yeah, but I feel kinda bad about hassling you about our journals. You know that 'So What? Now What?' stuff?" she says, again looking embarrassed.

"Are you telling me that it worked?" I ask, surprised.

"I realized how much more I was remembering, Mrs. Sprenger. So I started using it in all my classes. Many of those Bs I always get are becoming As. I think I needed to think more about what I was learning. I just want you to know that some of that brain stuff you talk about really works!"

I smile and thank her. She moves on to her class. I open my journal and begin a new page of "So What? Now What?" All I write is "Hooray!"

Reflection is not just the second step in this process of building memory. Reflection will be used throughout the entire process. It is wise to reflect after each step: after recoding, reinforcement, and each rehearsal. I tell my students that reflection is a form of rehearsal. They are ensuring their own memory success by using the reflection process.

Mental Note: Reflection is the first rehearsal.

A Time to Be Silent and a Time to Speak

As in comedy, one secret of good teaching is timing. A response delivered too early or too late may not have the effect we expect. If a teacher responds too quickly, students don't learn as well (Stahl, 1994; Tobin, 1987). Now is the time to examine moments when our students need our silence. Silence that encourages reflective thinking can eventually lead to long-term memory.

The ability to reflect critically on one's experience and combine that experience with prior knowledge is essential to take information from immediate memory to process it in active working memory. Keep in mind that active working memory allows us to hold onto incoming information while our brains search long-term memory for patterns or connections that it recognizes. According to Williamson (1997), reflective practice may be a developmental learning process, and Wellington (1996) considers the possibility of different levels of attainment. Taking these views into consideration, teaching our students about the value of reflection may be a first step toward a *habit* of reflection.

It seems that our biggest enemy in education is time. We don't have enough time to cover the curriculum. We don't have enough time to prepare for the state test. We don't have time to give individual attention to our students. And, we barely have time to eat lunch, go to the restroom, and check our e-mail before classes begin again!

When we are not doing two things at once, we must be wasting time. Educators talk about downtime, "wait" time, extra time, overtime, and now time for reflection. Where do we find the time?

The simple answer is that if we don't take the time to do many of these things, long-term retention will not be possible. In this chapter, we will look at focus time, wait time, and time for reflection.

Mental Note: Make time to take time.

Focus Time

According to research (e.g., DeFina, 2003), focus time for our students is their age in minutes. On a good day, 10-year-olds can give you 10 minutes of focus on a given stimulus. If you are having a long group discussion with this age group, you would probably see students looking for other types of stimulation. Students may start having private conversations, moving around, or finding something else to do. This is a natural occurrence. When the stimulation we are getting exceeds our capacity for concentration, the area of the brain expending energy on the task is running out of steam or, in this case, glucose.

Imagine working busily at your computer. You may be writing a report for a class, an article for a journal, or working on a grant proposal. Suddenly, you can't focus your eyes very well, and you become "brain dead"—you can't think of a thing. Some have described this feeling as "hitting a wall." Your brain is tired, and it needs to rest. Perhaps you get up and find something else to do. You might rest for a few minutes, go to the refrigerator for a snack, or even shoot some baskets. After a few minutes, you feel better and can go back to your project.

Your students go through the same biological process. The difference, however, is that students must follow rules, such as: no talking, no getting out of your seat, and no snacking. Therefore, they will give you subtle hints at first, but if you ignore the simple movements and quiet conversations and continue on the same track, the symptoms of a tired brain will become less subtle. Their brains are telling them to do something else, to use another area.

According to Perry (2000), presentations must weave themselves between neural systems. He believes that neurons fatigue in four to eight minutes. This is a bit less than age in minutes. Perry suggests we begin teaching by tapping into emotions, by telling a story. Then add some facts (semantic information), followed by some conceptual understandings that relate back to the original story. This strategy will keep the neural systems aroused without draining all of their energy.

> **Mental Note: Changing the sensory stimulation you give students within their focus time will make lessons unproblematic.**

Wait Time

> Slowing down may be a way of speeding up.
>
> —*Mary Budd Rowe, "Wait Time"*

In the late 1960s, Mary Budd Rowe scrutinized instruction by teachers in a wide assortment of classroom settings. She established that teachers asked questions of students at the rate of two or three per minute. Only one second would pass before the questions were repeated or reshaped or before the teacher called on someone else. If students did respond quickly enough, the teacher then replied on average within 0.9 second by asking another question or responding to the given answer (Rowe, 1973).

For many of us, wait time is not a new idea, but it plays a vital role in the retention process. Offering students the opportunity to have just a few seconds to respond can give them enough reflective time to access prior knowledge, evaluate what has been said, and formulate an appropriate response.

According to Rowe, there are two wait-time intervals. The first is the interlude between a person's asking a question and not receiving a response and changing the question, asking a probing question, calling on another student, or answering the question himself. The second is the break after receiving a response and before saying anything. For the first interval, the average teacher waits 0.9 seconds. The wait for the second interval is usually even shorter. When these intervals are increased to at least three seconds, some remarkable changes occurred for the students (see Figure 2.1). Other more general effects are also noticeable: classroom discipline improves, teachers ask fewer and better questions (requiring higher-order thinking skills), and expectations for all students are raised (Rowe, 1986).

Where in a lesson can wait time be beneficial?

- Upon asking an initial question and prior to calling on a student or group of students for a response.

Figure 2.1
Impact of Wait Time as Determined by Rowe (1986)

- **Responses change in length from a single word to whole statements.**
- **Self-confidence increases.**
- **Speculative thinking increases.**
- **The questioning tone of the responses decreases.**
- **Guessing, "I don't know," and inappropriate responses decrease.**
- **Students "piggyback" on each other's ideas.**
- **Responses by "slow" students increase.**
- **The interaction becomes a student–student discussion, moderated by the teacher, instead of a teacher–student inquisition.**
- **Students ask more questions.**
- **Students propose more investigations.**
- ***Student achievement improves.***

- Following the response from a student or group of students to the initial question.

- Subsequent to receiving a student's question and prior to responding.

- After asking a follow-up question.

Fogarty (1997) suggests two verbal responses to keep students thinking about an idea or concept. The first is "What else?" This question conveys to other students that there may be other acceptable answers and to keep trying. The other statement is "Tell me more." This request cues the students to do more in-depth thinking, to dig for details, and to synthesize information.

Mental Note: Students need time to answer and to question.

Other Times to "Wait"

Stahl (1994) suggests other periods of silence that he calls "think time." Using the research of Rowe and others, he has some additional situations for applying wait time. *Teacher pause-time* is distinguished by a three-second or more period of uninterrupted silence to consider what just took place, what the present situation is, and what their next statements or behaviors could and should be. *Impact pause-time* is an attention getter when the teacher pauses for several seconds or even minutes, allowing the students to realize the silence and to get back on task. *Within–student's response pause-time* is an interval of time when a student pauses while giving an answer. Most teachers are uncomfortable with the pause and begin helping the student. Stahl suggests allowing at least three seconds here. *Post–student's response wait-time* is a silence of three seconds or more given to allow other students to think about the response and respond to it.

I have just asked Jonathon to contribute to the discussion this junior class is having on the topic of culture. We are answering the fact-based question, "What are the cultural universals?"

Jonathon begins, "I think all cultures . . . ." He pauses to think (within–student's response pause). Perhaps I have caught him off-guard, or this could be a process that he is not accustomed to. Some students start to snicker; others raise their hands to take over. I give those laughing one of my "looks" and turn my attention back to Jonathon.

He continues, "Yes, I definitely think all cultures have rules about what's right and what's wrong. Different ones, but they all have them."

I start to lift my marker to add the category. Before I start writing Jonathon's answer on the board, Jeffrey speaks. "Every person has his own sense of right and wrong," he says. "Let's find out what each person in this class considers acceptable."

I hesitate. I need time to decide whether I want to open this can of worms (teacher pause-time). Do I want to take this idea and run with it? Are my students comfortable enough with each other and with me to open up? The students appear excited about this idea. "OK," I begin. "Everyone make a list of your own of what you think is unacceptable behavior."

Teacher pause-time appears to be a luxury in our hectic schedules, but taking that time to consider or change the course of events in a lesson can be very helpful. Many of us do not use student pause-time for two reasons. First, we don't want to embarrass the student; we feel that by waiting for answers or questions that we are putting students on the spot. Second, our students are so accustomed to what I call "video game" responses that we worry about keeping them all on task. Perhaps we are underestimating all of our students when we fall into these traps.

Hurry Up and Wait!

In the beginning, wait time may feel awkward to you and your students. Keep in mind that lower-level questions require less wait time, and higher-level questions may take 5 to 10 minutes. In the latter case, expect all students to be pondering the question. Acknowledge students who are ready with an answer, but do not interrupt the waiting period. Give your students those seconds they need. The silence may be uncomfortable, so count or check the second hand on your watch as you wait for time to pass. Better yet, count the number of "aha!" looks on your students' faces. When you accept responses, refrain from commenting on answers. A simple "thank you" acknowledges a contribution without giving verbal rewards.

Imagine yourself searching long-term memory for a name, a book title, or a phone number. You are scanning all sorts of information tucked neatly away in your brain. Now imagine being interrupted by someone talking while you are searching. Better yet, imagine someone interrupting your thoughts with an answer you were trying to find yourself. Frustrating, huh? That's why wait time is so important. Some of us need a bit more time than others to access information.

> **Mental Note: Wait time allows students to search their long-term memory while holding onto new information.**

Reflection

Studies have been completed that examine some of the neurocognitive processes underlying reflection using MRI or PET (positron emission tomography—tracking the amount of energy being used by areas of the brain) scans (Johnson et al., 2002). The results show that reflection is processed in the frontal lobes of the brain. The implications here are that reflection is done in the most advanced brain areas, sometimes referred to as the executive area of the brain. Working memory is also processed here.

Atkins and Murphy (1993) have identified three stages in the reflective process. An awareness of uncomfortable feelings is followed by a critical analysis of the situation and, finally, the development of a new perspective relating to the situation. Burrows (1995) defines the process of reflecting as an "exploration and discovery to make sense of new information and leads on to a process of critical reflection, reframing problems and identifying probable consequences" (p. 346). Kemmis's (1985) description of the process differs. He views the reflective process as analytical, focusing inward on one's own thoughts and processes and focusing outward at the situation one is involved with. From the learner's perspective, Boud, Keough, and Walker (1985) say that reflection is a combination of intellectual and affective activities in which students engage to explore their experiences, leading them to a new understanding. Dewey (1997) states, "Reflection—thought in its best sense . . . is turning a topic over in various aspects and in various lights so that nothing significant about it shall be overlooked—almost as one might turn a stone over to see what its hidden side is like or what is covered by it" (p. 57).

With my students, I like to explain reflection as a chance not only to make connections with something they may already know but to question the source—whether it is me, the author of their text, or any other source. I ask them to be detectives to get to the heart of the matter, and I suggest that their hearts (their feelings and opinions) are important.

Reflection time is not what has been called downtime. *Downtime* refers to the time of day when the brain is less likely to take in information (Erlauer, 2003). Rather, reflection takes place in lessons and units throughout the school day.

Perkins (1995) refers to three intelligences: neural intelligence, experiential intelligence, and reflective intelligence. The first is the contribution of neural efficiency to intelligent behavior—in other words, how well the brain makes and keeps connections. Experiential intelligence encompasses the personal experiences we have that contribute to intelligent behavior. Knowledge, understanding, and attitudes about how our minds should be used constitute reflective intelligence. Perkins states that the second two, experiential and reflective, are learnable intelligences. He considers reflective intelligence as the control system for the other intelligences.

The consensus is that reflection can be and must be taught. The question is, How? What are good reflective practices? In *Connecting the Brain to Leadership*, Dickman and Blair (2002) state that "the reflective nature of intelligence can be interpreted as the conscious bending back of information patterns to discern potential relationships of peril or promise" (p. 96). They add that a reflection task requires five areas:

- **Physiological.** Your brain literally lights up with activity as you reflect. The more novel the item of reflection, the more activity is present.

- **Social.** Reflection promotes social experience as the brain seeks out other brains.

- **Emotional.** Evaluation is part of the reflective process. To value something worth your reflection, emotion must be involved.

- **Constructive.** Knowledge is constructed during the reflective process. New patterns of thinking may be assembled as well as old patterns retrieved.
- **Dispositional.** From these new patterns, habits may be formed.

Mental Note: Reflection is a learned habit.

The Seven Habits of Highly Reflective Classrooms

OK, so I borrowed a catchy phrase from Stephen Covey's work, *The Seven Habits of Highly Effective People*. But the point is, it may help you remember that there are at least seven strategies that, when used purposefully and often, may become habits for you and your students. According to Costa and Kallick (2000), thinking about our thinking is one of the 16 habits of mind. "Intelligent people," they say, "plan for, reflect on, and evaluate the quality of their own thinking skills and strategies" (p. 5).

We want our students to be aware of their skills, strategies, and experiences. According to Cohen (1999) in *Educating Minds and Hearts*, "I would suggest that self-reflective capacities on the one hand and the ability to recognize what others are thinking and feeling on the other provide the foundation for children to understand, manage, and express the social and emotional aspects of life" (p. 11).

Habit 1: Question

Questioning is at the heart of reflection. According to Marzano, Pickering, Norford, Paynter, and Gaddy (2001), who describe questioning as being either inferential or analytical, questions should focus on what is important, rather than what is unusual. Johnson (1995) labels questions as follows: quantity questions, compare/contrast questions, feelings/opinions/point of view/personification questions, "What if?" questions, and "How come?" questions. She then further categorizes questioning as passive or active. *Active* questions are those that students ask; *passive* are those they answer. In the reflective process, we want them to do both: ask themselves questions and search for the answers. The importance of this activity cannot be understated, but in order for students to get into this habit, the teacher must model questioning.

Fogarty (1997) refers to "fat" questions and "skinny" questions. *Fat* questions require discussion and explanation with examples, whereas *skinny* questions require simple yes/no responses. Jacobs (1997) discusses the concept of essential questions. These questions are meant to refine and organize the curriculum in the classroom.

Reflective questions often start with *why* or *how*. When you offer your students these questions, you are inviting them to ask themselves, "How do I know what I know?" Asking factual questions such as "Who?" "When?" or "Where?" will not lead them to the connections they can discover through the more thought-provoking and higher-level questions. For instance, after reaching her students by dressing in a Tooth Fairy costume, the health teacher shared some facts and concepts about dental health. For reflection using the questioning habit, she asked, "How does my smile affect my life?"

Choose a questioning technique, and get into the habit of using it. When you began with the end in mind, you devised several essential questions for your unit. Ask students one of these reflective questions as you introduce material, and then offer it to them again for their reflection. Do this often enough, and they will begin to ask themselves extension questions. Then the habit will be set!

> **Mental Note: Albert Einstein said, "The important thing is not to stop questioning."**

Habit 2: Visualize

A picture is worth a thousand words, or so the saying goes. Students who can visualize can temporarily store a lot of information in that relatively small space known as working memory. According to Howard Gardner's 1983 thesis on multiple intelligences, most people possess a visual/spatial intelligence. The ability to make use of this intelligence while receiving information in other forms affords the possibility of multiple coding, which is an area that needs to be strengthened in all students. PET scans show that visual information causes a great deal of brain activity in the right hemisphere (Burmark, 2002).

Expecting your students to be able to visualize regardless of their learning preferences seems like an intrusion. But in my experience of using mind mapping as a memory tool, I saw all kinds of learners visualizing their maps to retrieve information.

It is interesting how different visual pictures emerge from our students. I have often had my students draw the picture they mentally created. Then we would share pictures and discuss the different perceptions of the material. In fact, for young students, drawing what they visualize may be a necessity.

We all have visual schemas or mental maps that we use on a regular basis (Armstrong, 1993). These episodic memory maps get us where we are going. Reminders of role models who use similar strategies may encourage your students to try it. For example, many of the sports fans in my classes knew that professional athletes use visualization techniques. Mark McGwire, for one, is a strong hitter who uses visualization to practice his sport. He knows that the brain actually allows you to practice mentally and improve your performance (Gamon & Bragdon, 2001). Albert Einstein, Charles Darwin, and Sigmund Freud also used visual thinking—images to conjure up their theories. For example, Einstein pictured what it would be like to ride on a beam of light. From that visual, he moved on to his theory of relativity.

Get your students started on visualization by having them put down on paper some of those visual maps already stored in their memories. They could

- Draw a map from home to school.

- Create a map of the United States.

- Draw a picture of the inside of a computer.

- Draw a picture of a concept, such as freedom.

- Create a blueprint of the school or your classroom.

- Play Pictionary.

- Create symbols for certain concepts, such as a torch for freedom.

Once they realize that they have these mental pictures in their heads, encourage them to use their visualization powers to reflect on new information.

Habit 3: Thinking Through Journals

Seven thousand notebook pages belonging to Leonardo da Vinci still exist. He always carried a notebook with him. He wrote down everything: ideas, observations, jokes, and plans for new inventions (Gelb, 1998).

Have your students keep a journal. Reflection time can involve writing questions, observations, connections to prior knowledge, or any insights into the lesson presented. If you have reached your students—that is, if they have been attending to you and the class—they will have something to record in their journals.

According to current research, writing about an experience provides a feeling of control (Restak, 2000). Reflection stems may be helpful in the beginning:

- I learned . . . .
- I want to learn more about . . . .
- I liked . . . .
- I did not like . . . .
- I did not understand . . . .
- I would have liked (or understood) it better if . . . .

Habit 4: Use Thinking Directives

Give your students time to think about the information they have received. There are many approaches to thinking. The following are some possibilities, but think creatively:

- Think about . . . .
- Think back to a time . . . .
- Think to the future when . . . .
- Put yourself in someone else's shoes. What would they think about . . . ?
- Think reproductively (how has this happened before?).
- Think productively (how many ways can I approach this?).
- Think of a comparison, analogy, or metaphor.

Habit 5: Think Like a PMI Chart

A PMI chart is a graphic organizer that will give students an organized reflection time. The *P* stands for *plus*: What part of what we just covered is positive for you? The *M* stands for *minus*: Are there topics or concepts that you don't like or understand? *I* represents *interesting*: What parts of this lesson do you find interesting?

The PMI chart can be set up horizontally or vertically. If your students use this chart several times, they may then be able to think using the categories. You may also substitute *implications* for *interesting*, which may be a good alternative for older students. (See Appendix B for examples of this and other graphic organizers.)

Habit 6: Collaborate

The skills involved in working together must be established for this habit to be successful. If you have taught emotional intelligence skills as an avenue for reaching your students as discussed in Chapter 1, then your students should be able to handle the task of reflecting with others.

At the 2004 ASCD Annual Conference, I had the pleasure to listen to Margaret Wheatley (2004) speak on the topic of her recent book, *Turning to One Another: Simple Conversations to Restore Hope to the Future.* She commented that in our present society, we are trying to get humans to work at the same speed as machines. "We are losing our time to think. We are losing our time to be together." She suggested that we reclaim the time we need to reflect, listen, and understand each other. Collaborating during the reflective step gives our students the opportunity to do so.

Johnson, Johnson, and Holubec (1994) have identified five elements of cooperative learning. The process of cooperative collaboration is exemplified by students (1) knowing that they are "in this together," (2) helping each other learn and celebrating successes, (3) taking responsibility for contributions, (4) building group skills such as conflict resolution, and (5) reflecting on group and individual processing.

These authors encourage monitoring collaboration, and Tileston (2000) suggests "cruise control." The teacher must cruise the room to keep students on task. This is also the first opportunity to check for understanding. As the students share their reflections, you may be able to catch misconceptions. Interrupting the collaboration may be an option, or you may take time after the reflective collaboration to make some clarifications. Figure 2.2. cites a procedure for reflective collaboration; Figure 2.3 presents a rubric for collaboration.

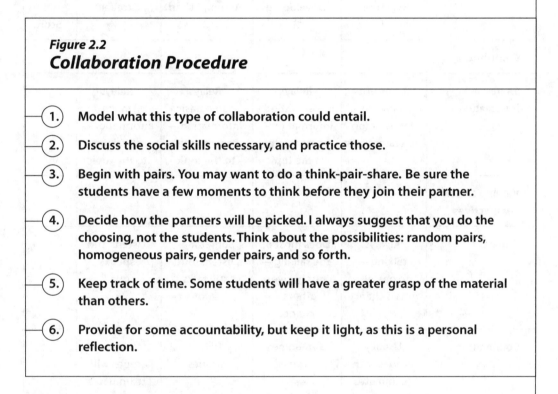

Figure 2.2
Collaboration Procedure

1. Model what this type of collaboration could entail.

2. Discuss the social skills necessary, and practice those.

3. Begin with pairs. You may want to do a think-pair-share. Be sure the students have a few moments to think before they join their partner.

4. Decide how the partners will be picked. I always suggest that you do the choosing, not the students. Think about the possibilities: random pairs, homogeneous pairs, gender pairs, and so forth.

5. Keep track of time. Some students will have a greater grasp of the material than others.

6. Provide for some accountability, but keep it light, as this is a personal reflection.

Habit 7: Four-Corner Reflection

This multimodal approach to reflecting may incorporate movement, music, discussion, and visuals. Here's how it works:

1. Place charts with key ideas covered in the four corners of the room.

2. Have students gather in groups in each corner to discuss the topic and generate ideas and opinions.

3. Have chart paper on an easel or otherwise attached to a wall for the students to write their reflections.

Figure 2.3
Sample Rubric for Reflective Collaboration

	Beginning 1	Developing 2	Accomplished 3	Excellent 4	Score
Contributing					
Share information	Does not relay any information to teammates	Relays very little information— some relates to the topic	Relays some basic information— most relates to the topic	Relays much information— all relates to the topic	
Valuing Others' Perspectives					
Listens	Always talking— no one else gets a chance	Does most of the talking— rarely gives others a chance	Sometimes listens, but still talks a lot	Listens and speaks equally	
Cooperation	Usually argues with teammates	Sometimes argues	Rarely argues	Never argues with teammates	
				Total	

4. After five minutes, play music or blow a whistle to signal the students that it is time to go to the next corner.

5. Let each group add to the previous list of ideas or reflections.

6. The last group at a given corner is responsible for summarizing the information generated.

7. Engage in whole-group discussion.

As you get into the habit of offering students reflection time, you may need to be selective. Your content may dictate which reflective habit you choose. For instance, when our students do an interdisciplinary unit on the Holocaust, many students become quite emotional. If they have personal connections, discussion may be too invasive. Questioning or thinking through journals may be better habits to follow, at least initially. On the other hand, a science unit on the weather may be perfect for a four-corner reflection with different weather conditions displayed.

> **Mental Note: As adults we reflect as we learn. Organizing the reflection through one of the habits helps young people make connections with prior knowledge as they mentally arrange what they have received.**

Teacher Reflection

It is important that teachers receive or provide themselves with reflection time. The authors of *Schools That Learn* (Senge et al., 2000) consider three different components of reflection:

- **Reconsider.** Question yourself. Are you getting your points across? Are your expectations where they should be? Challenge your assumptions and conclusions.

- **Reconnect.** Who else has attempted this in a different way? Look at trends, data, and methods of implementation.

- **Reframe.** Do some scenario planning, incorporating diverse possibilities. Imagine yourself and your students in each scenario.

According to Stronge (2002), reflection is an element of professionalism. Research on the value of reflection includes findings that effective teachers may reflect formally or informally, students with high achievement rates have teachers who use reflection on their work as an important component for improvement, and teachers who reflect maintain high expectations for students.

Mental Note: Teachers who use and model reflective practice will have a better understanding of and higher expectations for their students' reflective capabilities.

Reflection as Assessment

These reflection habits are informal assessments. While your students are reflecting and you are on cruise control, gather as much information as you can. Your students' reflections will offer you the information you need to determine whether they are ready for the next step in the process: recoding. You may want to determine whether they can make connections by using an assessment rubric for the seven habits (see Figure 2.4).

I am introducing comparison/contrast writing. I have donned my Minnie Mouse costume, and the students chuckle as they enter the room. I have a stuffed Mickey Mouse and Donald Duck on the overhead table. As I explain the procedure for doing this form of expression, we compare and contrast Mickey and Donald. This is a simple task for my students, but that is what I want. I want their working memories to concentrate on the form of this writing, rather than taxing their brains for the similarities and differences.

We are successful at completing the essay. The emotion and novelty helped me reach my students. It was a short piece, so I was able to keep them attentive throughout. I wrote the similarities in red marker and the differences in green. The colors seemed to intrigue some of the students.

Time for reflection. I call on habit 2, visualization. "I want you to visualize two other characters that you can compare and contrast using only physical characteristics. Picture them in your mind, and make a mental list of what those similarities and differences are." I give the students five minutes for reflection. Most of them seem to be making connections. Some are nodding, some are laughing. Others look very serious. A few students don't seem to get it.

"Let's reflect a little more and get a concrete look at this. Take a sheet of paper and draw your characters. As you compare physical characteristics, draw arrows to them."

Figure 2.4
Assessment Rubric for Reflection. Students scoring a 3 or 4 are ready for step 3, Recoding.

Reflective Habit	1	2	3	4	Score
	The student has	The student has	The student has	The student has	
Questioning	No questions answered or generated	Questions generated are unrelated; questions answered don't relate	One related question	Several related questions	
Visualizing Picture	No picture	Unrelated picture	A drawing	Ability to describe her mental picture	
Journal	Little or no writing	Unrelated writing	Repetition of what was said	Connections between prior knowledge and new information	
Thinking Directives	No directives	Unrelated thoughts	Follows directive	Follows directive and goes beyond	
PMI	No chart	Incomplete information	Completed chart	Completed mental chart	
Collaboration	No participation	Little participation	Short discussion	Obvious understanding through discussion	
Four Corner	No interaction or notes	Little interaction; few notes	Some interaction; some notes	Obvious understanding through interaction and notes	

All students get busy on this project. Those students who did not seem to be able to reflect visually or simply did not understand the lesson are beginning to apply what was covered. I have the opportunity now to cruise the room and determine whether we need to create another group essay or whether they are ready to write their own.

Mental Note: The process of reflecting can be affected by learning style, emotional states, or specific content. Be prepared to kick one habit for another.

Thinking About Information in Working Memory

Belmont, Butterfield, and Ferretti (cited in Perkins, 1995) concluded after reviewing studies on teaching strategies to retarded learners that these students would transfer memory strategies to other settings and circumstances *if they were taught self-monitoring strategies along with the memory strategies*. The strategy they were taught was questioning.

Thinking about our thinking is a necessary skill for life-long learning. Reflective habits lead us to a better understanding of how our brains work. Students need to have the ability and skills to plan, monitor, and evaluate their thinking. This leads to controlling thinking and behavior. Knowing how and why we think the way we do is *metacognition*, which leads to applying thinking skills in new situations.

Thus far in our discussion, students have been reached through sensory and immediate memory and are now manipulating the facts and concepts in working memory. As they strive to make connections, they are rehearsing the new learning and finding ways to attach it to prior knowledge.

Reflection

1. Some students respond better to concrete reflection; that is, they need to do it in order to see it. Be ready to shift gears when a reflection piece isn't working for everyone.

2. With the emphasis in most schools on coverage and testing, reflection seems like an extravagance. Keep in mind that this is the step that can make the difference in reaching accessible memories. It marks the beginning of ownership of the information.

3. Some students may overreflect and overanalyze certain material or situations, which is why time limits are important for these sessions. Others may not have a handle on the material and be unable to do much reflection. Too much time allows them to disrupt others.

4. Whichever practice you use for your students' reflection, keep in mind that you are allowing the brain time to make associations.

Recode

Self-generated material is better recalled.

> You don't know anything clearly unless you can state it in writing.
>
> —S. I. Hayakawa, Language in Thought and Action

It is the week before the start of the new school year. I am having my "movie marathon." I gather the movies that inspire me: Mr. Holland's Opus, Stand and Deliver, Dead Poet's Society, and Dangerous Minds are a few. Watching movies such as these inspire me for the job ahead. It is easy to get sidetracked at the beginning of the year by paperwork, heat, new curricula, and new rules.

In the midst of watching Dangerous Minds, I have a brainstorm. It dawns on me what I have been neglecting to do with my students to increase their memories. As Lou Ann Johnson, the teacher in the movie, is introducing poetry to her students, she says, "It's written in code. You have to break the code."

Our students are constantly trying to break a code. A textbook code. A lecture code. A video code. An Internet site code. Language varies from vehicle to vehicle. Student's understanding of language changes according to their backgrounds.

I feel as though I have discovered a memory fixative. If my students can "break the code" and recode the information in their own language, not only will they have a better understanding of it; they will also have a better *memory* of it.

What Is Recoding?

Recoding is the ability to take information from different sources and generate it in your own language. It can be symbolic, as in drawing pictures or constructing through movement. Let's keep in mind, however, that when our students are tested, they must have the ability to share information linguistically. At some point in this seven-step process, therefore, information must be manipulated through paper and pencil.

According to Levine (2002), some students who have trouble recoding are experiencing short-term memory problems. He defines *recoding* as the ability to summarize and paraphrase. Levine suggests that we encourage students to use their strongest sensory pathway in order to work with this problem.

I agree with Hayakawa's quote at the beginning of this chapter. If students can write about what they know, then we know they know it. In first learning new concepts, some students may have more difficulty with writing and need to use a different mode of expression. This calls for differentiation—meeting learners where they are and offering them appropriate and challenging options to achieve success (Tomlinson, 1999). If we are truly differentiating our classrooms, then we should permit some choice in the recoding process. After the students can show their understanding, it is time for them to stretch to another medium (Sprenger, 2003). Because our instruction is covering standards that will be assessed on a paper-and-pencil test, it behooves us to encourage students to work on using their semantic pathways, perhaps even insisting they do so.

Mental Note: Self-generated material is better remembered.

Why Recode?

I am delivering a presentation on memory to about 1,400 people. "Stand up if you have something good to say about your memory," I begin. A dozen people stand.

"Raise your hand if you lose your keys," I say next. All hands are raised on this one.

"But how many of you have a specific spot in your home or office where you always put your keys?" Again all hands. "Except when you don't!" Laughter and nodding follow.

"Believe me, I have been tempted to call the psychic hotline more than once to find out where those darn keys are," I tell the audience. "Memory research will make us all feel better. You see, you can't retrieve information that you haven't stored. When your keys aren't where they are supposed to be, it's because you have so many things on your mind that you didn't pay attention to where you put them. You didn't use the typical organizational model that you usually do. That's why tracing your steps will often work."

Most memory experts (e.g., Small, 2002) suggest that organization is the key to a good memory. Systematically arranging information according to groups, patterns, and other structures in an effective manner can make the difference between success and failure with storage and retrieval of information.

In my seminars, I test this hypothesis: I read a list of about 10 words. Before the participants write down the words they remember, I try to delay them for a matter of seconds. Following the primacy-recency effect, which tells us that we remember beginnings and endings more than middles, most people cannot write down every word. When I then read the *category* that the words might fit in, they often make that connection and retrieve the words (see Figure 3.1 for an example of this technique). I emphasize to the group how important it is to show their students ways to organize information.

According to Engle, Kane, and Tuholski (1999), people with higher working memory capacity do better on standardized college admission tests, intelligence tests, and reading comprehension tests. Research from the Social Cognitive Laboratory at North Carolina State University strongly suggests that writing can affect working memory capacity in general. The study used three groups: One group wrote about a positive experience, one wrote about a negative experience, and the

Figure 3.1
Organizing by Category to Remember 20 Words

Apple	Car
Hammer	Pear
Train	Rose
Orange	Wrench
Lily	Squirrel
Daisy	Airplane
Zebra	Lion
Tulip	Pliers
Saw	Camel
Cherry	Boat

Fruit	Animals	Flowers	Transportation	Tools
Apple	Squirrel	Rose	Car	Hammer
Pear	Camel	Lily	Train	Wrench
Orange	Zebra	Tulip	Airplane	Pliers
Cherry	Lion	Daisy	Boat	Saw

last group wrote about daily activities. Working memory improved in all three groups (Klein & Boals, 2001).

Other research supports the effects of self-generated material. Bruning, Schraw, and Ronning (1999) demonstrated that when students generate their own context for meaning, memory improves. Research on the generation effect (Rabinowitz & Craik, 1986) consistently shows that students do better when they make their own meaning.

When we go back to the memory processes, self-generation makes sense. The students create their own understanding, which involves taking explicit, semantic material and coding it in a personal way. This adds some implicit memory to the process. If true understanding takes place, emotions are involved. The process of recoding in some cases will involve movement and perhaps a procedural component. All of this strengthens the possibilities for long-term retention.

Organization is significant in the recoding process of factual information. Our brains will organize information, but if we are not in control of that organization, we may have difficulty accessing the memory. Recoding offers the opportunity for students to organize thoughts, facts, and concepts in a format that is conducive not only with the way their brains think but also with the specific type of material.

When information will be accessed in the same way repeatedly and does not require learning a concept, the organization process may be quite different. For instance, we learn the multiplication tables and are expected to retrieve them in an automatic fashion and in the same way each time. Although we learn them in a rote fashion, understanding the concepts behind the learning is essential.

Organization can be a problem for some students. They may have trouble finding the materials they need, managing their time to get things done, managing complex tasks, prioritizing, and organizing their thoughts (Levine, 2003). The recoding experience will offer them strategies, sometimes called *mental models* or *schemata*, that will be useful in many situations.

 Mental Note: Memories for intentional learning require intentional organization.

What Are We Recoding?

Information that has been received and reflected upon is developed for recoding. This may include factual knowledge, conceptual knowledge, or procedural knowledge. After studying a revision of Bloom's Taxonomy of Educational Objectives, *A Taxonomy for Learning, Teaching, and Assessing* (Anderson et al., 2001), I learned the following:

- Recoding falls into the cognitive process category of understanding for conceptual knowledge—constructing meaning from instructional messages, including oral, written, and graphic communication.

- Procedural knowledge is in the process category—applying, carrying out, or using a procedure in a given situation.

- Factual knowledge is under the category "Remember." Recoding allows us to assess the perceptions and comprehension our students have of the content being covered. In some instances, the significance of the content to the student may also be derived from this practice.

How Do We Recode Factual Knowledge?

Factual knowledge includes terminology and details. This is information that needs to be remembered in much the same form that it is taught. Knowing this information may be an important basis for conceptual and procedural learning. According to Sternberg, Grigorenko, and Jarvin (2001), "One cannot analyze what one knows (analytical thinking), go beyond what one knows (creative thinking), or apply what one knows (practical thinking) if one does not know anything" (p. 48).

Recoding this information may encompass different processes. For some students, writing the information several times may help, as in learning spelling words. Others may use oral repetition. Creating symbols, songs, or movements may help others.

We can look at vocabulary as one type of factual knowledge. Research demonstrates that vocabulary words need to be taught through direct instruction. In order for our students to better understand words in context, they need to be introduced to them in advance. This research also suggests that associating an image with a word is the best way to learn it (Marzano, Pickering, & Pollack, 2001). Here is a suggested procedure for teaching vocabulary:

1. Choose words that are critical to the content.

2. Introduce those words and their meanings with your own image to represent each one.

3. Let students reflect on those meanings and images.

4. Ask students to create an image to associate with each word.

Mental Note: Factual information is a basis for conceptual understanding.

How Do We Recode Conceptual Knowledge?

Seven cognitive processes assist in constructing meaning from instructional messages (Anderson et al., 2001). These are to be used when we want our students to be able not only to remember but also to transfer information and eventually use it in unanticipated situations. The seven processes are listed below:

- Interpreting
- Exemplifying
- Classifying
- Summarizing
- Inferring
- Comparing
- Explaining

Research strongly suggests that many of these strategies will raise student achievement. They may be used at the recoding stage and again at the rehearsal stage.

Interpreting

In the clearest sense of the word, *recoding* is interpreting, or the ability to change information from one form into another. Whenever our students take notes when we speak, they are interpreting our words, unless they are writing what we say verbatim.

The subcategories of interpreting include paraphrasing, clarifying, and translating. Paraphrasing

- Involves putting a passage from a source into your own words,

- Changes the words or phrasing of a spoken or written passage but retains and fully communicates the original meaning, and

- Must be attributed to the original source.

Many students will gain from direct instruction in interpreting (Olivier & Bowler, 1996). Interpretations may take many forms. A student could paraphrase a famous speech, draw an illustration of the process of mitosis, write a mathematical equation from a story problem, or create a dance to translate the feelings of the Pilgrims or the Indians. We want to prepare our students to apply their interpretations in other situations as will be expected of them in the real world and on standardized tests.

Stiggins (2001) suggests interpretive exercises for assessment. Offer a brief passage, table, or chart, and ask a series of questions that calls for interpretation of the material.

Exemplifying

Exemplification is a communication practice through which meaning is explained by the use of linguistic forms called *examples*. Examples can be defined in several ways. They may be thought of in terms of representatives of a group, a pattern of a specific kind, a similar case that comprises a precedent, or a problem or exercise used to explain a principle or a concept.

Finding examples is a task that many students enjoy. A common assignment while studying geometry is to define and discuss angles; students are then sent out on a "field trip" in the building to find such angles. For instance, the glass panels in the doors of the building may have right angles. Using principles and concepts, students begin finding their own examples.

According to Kahn (2002), a good set of examples will include simple examples, typical examples, and unusual examples, and it will be complemented by some nonexamples. While *simple* examples are self-explanatory, *typical* examples contain all of the characteristics of the idea with nothing left out. *Unusual* examples indicate that the student can "step outside the box" and really understands the material. *Nonexamples* clarify understanding; when a student knows what does not qualify as an example, she has a better idea of the concept. A graphic organizer may be used for exemplifying; Appendix B has examples.

Storytelling can be part of exemplifying. Students love to tell stories, and stories can include patterns that represent the important components of the principle or concept. According to Damasio (1999), telling stories "is probably a brain obsession and probably begins relatively early both in terms of evolution and in terms of the complexity. Telling stories precedes language, since it is, in fact, a condition for language, and it is based not just in the cerebral cortex but elsewhere in the brain and in the right hemisphere as well as the left" (p. 189). In *Making Connections: Teaching and the Human Brain*, Caine and Caine (1994) state that "there is strong reason to believe that organization of information in story form is a natural brain process" (p. 122). Why fight Mother Nature? If this form of exemplifying will work with your content, encourage your students to recode using stories.

Illustrations are another way to exemplify. Fifty-five experiments were performed comparing learning from illustrated and nonillustrated texts. The results indicated that illustrations increased interest, enjoyment, and understanding. It was calculated that groups using illustrated texts performed 36 percent better than groups using text alone (Burmark, 2002). Creating or finding illustrations to exemplify conceptual understanding may be especially important and helpful to visual and kinesthetic learners.

Classifying

The ability to conceive that something fits into a particular category requires understanding the distinguishing features of it. According to Anderson and associates (2001), classifying and exemplifying are complementary abilities. To exemplify, one begins with a general concept or principle and leads the student to a more specific occurrence. Classifying takes the specific example and leads the student to the general concept or principle.

Classification tasks may be teacher directed or student directed. In *teacher-directed* tasks, the students are given the elements to classify as well as the categories for classification. When they recode the information, they determine under which category each element falls and focus on figuring out why. In *student-directed* classification tasks, students must take elements and create the categories (Marzano, Pickering, & Pollack, 2001).

A recoding assignment that uses student-directed classification may look something like the following:

> Make a list of the Civil War heroes we just discussed. Create categories of your choosing, but make sure they relate to one of our goals, such as: "Students will understand key people involved in the Civil War."

A more teacher-directed classification task may look something like this:

> Make a list of the Civil War heroes we just discussed. Use the following categories to show that you understand the key people involved in the war: Affiliation, Position, and Battles Fought.

The student-directed classification requires higher cognitive processes, so it is quite possible to differentiate using this strategy. Give students who are ready for higher-level processes a student-directed classification project and students who are not at the same readiness level a teacher-directed project. Graphic organizers are very conducive to this type of recoding. T charts, mind maps, webs, and Venn diagrams (see Appendix B) are examples of organizers that may be helpful.

Can we make mistakes with our classifications? In other words, are some categories better than others? Absolutely. Consider a common problem: labeling files in your computer. Have you ever completed a file and thought of different names for it? At the time you name the file, you have in working memory plenty of information about the topic—so much that you are certain that you will have no problem finding the file with the clever title you have chosen. Later, when it is time to access the file, you search and search, but the name you used does not trigger those memories. You may have to check several files before you find what you need. Our brains are much the same as our computers. If the categories and classifications are not strong and explanatory, we may have difficulty storing and retrieving the information (Baddeley, 1999).

Classifying is included in the research on identifying similarities and differences (Marzano, Pickering, Norford, et al., 2001). The percentile gain in learning for students who had received lessons on similarities and differences was between 31 and 46 percent. For encouraging results like these, use the classification recoding strategy in the most opportune ways possible for your students.

Summarizing

This recoding strategy occurs when students construct a representation of information. It has a strong research base showing a percentile gain of up to 47 percent. There are two fundamentals of summarizing: filling in missing parts and translating information into an amalgamated form (Marzano, Pickering, & Pollack, 2001). Summarizing includes extracting themes and main ideas, a skill that is often assessed on standardized achievement tests. According to Levine (2002), "All kids need to strengthen their summarization skills" (p. 148).

If students can read one or more articles and create a summary of important concepts or ideas, they can use this skill in a variety of settings. It is important that students understand that they need to do the following to summarize:

- Take out information that is not important.
- Delete repetitive information.
- Combine single elements into one category (e.g., gold, silver, and nickel become metals).
- Create a topic sentence.

Summarizing Sample

Original

As children, boys and girls have hemispheric differences. Generally, the female brain develops with a larger left hemisphere. Males start out as young boys with a larger right hemisphere. The implications of this are interesting. As I stated earlier, we know that women tend to be more verbal than men are. In fact, female toddlers have a much larger vocabulary than the boys their age. If we look again at the functions of the two hemispheres, this all makes perfect sense. The left hemisphere has verbal language as one of its functions. If this part of the brain develops earlier in girls, it is no wonder that we surge ahead of the boys in terms of communication skills and vocabulary. A study that was conducted at the University of Buffalo compared the hemispheric differences between male and female infants. Amazingly enough, while the girls were listening and processing language in their left hemispheres, the boys used their right hemispheres. It seemed that the boys didn't begin to use their left hemispheres until 9 months of age. The girls had been making a lot of neural connections in the language areas for months before the boys got started.

Words Deleted

~~As children, boys and girls have hemispheric differences. Generally,~~ the female brain develops with a larger left hemisphere. Males ~~start out as young boys with a~~ larger right hemisphere. ~~The implications of this are interesting. As I stated earlier, we know that~~ women tend to be more verbal than men are. ~~In fact,~~ female toddlers have a much larger vocabulary than the boys their age. ~~If we look again at the functions of the two hemispheres, this all makes perfect sense.~~ The left hemisphere has verbal language ~~as one of its functions. If this part of the brain~~ develops earlier in girls, ~~it is no wonder that~~ we surge ahead of the boys in terms of communication skills and vocabulary. ~~A study that was conducted at~~ the University of Buffalo compared the hemispheric differences between male and female infants. ~~Amazingly enough,~~ while the girls were listening and processing language in their left hemispheres, the boys used their right hemispheres. ~~It seemed that the boys didn't begin to use their left hemispheres~~ until 9 months of age. ~~The girls had been making a lot of neural connections in the language areas for months before the boys got started.~~

Summary

There are differences in brain development in girls and boys. (New topic sentence.) *The female brain develops with a larger left hemisphere, which has verbal language, while the male brain develops with the right hemisphere larger. This may be the reason that women tend to be more verbal, and in fact, female toddlers have a larger vocabulary than boys their age. The University of Buffalo compared the hemispheric differences and found that girls listen and process language in their left hemisphere, while boys use their right until the age of 9 months.*

Your students may benefit from taking a speech such as Martin Luther King's "I Have a Dream" and summarizing sections with partners or groups to help them understand this process. Asking students to read a nonfiction selection from a text and creating an appropriate title also falls into this category. This is not a simple task for most students. The better they know and understand the content, the easier it is to summarize. Summary frames can help. Discussed in *A Handbook for Classroom Instruction That Works* (Marzano, Pickering, Norford, et al., 2001), these frames represent common patterns in the form of questions. They cover narratives, topic-restriction-illustration, definition, argumentation, problem or solution, and conversation.

Inferring

Inferring is the ability to come to a conclusion based on evidence. As a language arts teacher, I found this cognitive process to be one of the more difficult ones to teach my students and one that always was assessed on our state test. In language arts, the *theme* is the universal idea that the author is trying to share with the reader. Themes are rarely revealed in written form—they must be inferred. I found it helpful to differentiate between facts and inferences. *Facts* are something we can observe, and *inferences* are interpretations. Inferences may remain unresolved.

Students must learn to "read between the lines" to make inferences. A three-column chart may be used as a graphic organizer for inference, with the first column labeled "Facts" or "What I Know for Sure," the middle column designated "Questions" or "What I Wonder," and the third column marked "Inferences." The inference column may have statements that begin with *maybe* or *probably*. A two-column chart with the labels "Facts" (or "What I Can Observe or Know") and

"Inferences" (or "My Interpretation") will also suffice. Students enjoy doing detective work, so presenting inferences in that context may be a good approach to the topic.

Marzano, Pickering, Norford, Paynter, and Gaddy (2001) suggest using inferential questions such as these to fill in gaps:

- What particular emotional state does this person have?
- Where does this event usually take place?
- How is this thing usually used?

In *I Read It but I Don't Get It*, Tovani (2000) suggests that we first help students distinguish between opinions and an inference. Opinions may be based on fact, but we cannot assume so. They aren't sufficient when interpreting text. Ask students what words help them draw a conclusion. Define the following terms:

- *Predictions*: Logical guess based on facts confirmed or disproved by the text
- *Inference*: Logical conclusion based on text clues and background knowledge
- *Assumption*: Fact or statement that is taken for granted that may or may not be correct
- *Opinion*: Belief or conclusion not based on facts that can be knowledgeable or ridiculous because it is based on what one thinks and isn't verified

Harvey and Goudvis (2000) suggest playing charades with students as a means to understand inference. Discussing and reading body language and visual expressions are also helpful for students.

Comparing

Identifying similarities and differences is the *number one way* to raise student achievement, according to the results of a meta-analysis (an analysis that combines and analyzes the results from several studies). Four generalizations were made from the study (Marzano, 1998):

- Presenting students with explicit guidance in identifying similarities and differences enhances their understanding of and ability to use knowledge.

- Asking students to identify similarities and differences independently enhances students' understanding of and ability to use knowledge.

- Representing similarities and differences in graphic or symbolic form enhances students' understanding of and ability to use knowledge.

- Identification of similarities and differences can be accomplished in a variety of ways.

To be effective at comparing, students need to be able to see the defining characteristics on which to base the similarities and the differences. The graphic organizer commonly used for this strategy is the Venn diagram (see Appendix B). I used to encourage my students to think in these diagrams. The similarities are written in the center where the circles overlap; the differences or distinguishing characteristics are placed in the parts of each circle that do not intersect.

Metaphors and analogies also help students make comparisons. In both strategies, we can take an unfamiliar concept and equate it with a familiar one. I would begin teaching metaphors with a line from Shakespeare: "All the world's a stage." This metaphor is comparing two unlike items: world and stage. My students would work together, using a Venn diagram to discover how these two items are similar and different.

The most powerful metaphors were those that my students created themselves. I used the following general process:

1. Take the topic we are studying, and choose a topic you are interested in or know a lot about (e.g., weather and computers).

2. Define each of them (weather—the state of the atmosphere; computers—machines that perform calculations).

3. Determine how these two are alike in the accurate sense (they are both very changeable).

4. Determine how they are alike in more abstract terms (the weather can affect whether a computer can be used; i.e., a storm).

Analogies are usually set up as "A is to B as C is to D." Those of us who had to take the Miller Analogies Test are quite familiar with the concept. We want to create a statement that suggests that two things are related to each other in the same way that two other things are related to each other—for example, fish : swim::bird : fly.

If students can create their own analogies, the complexity of the relationships helps them understand the concepts. There are many different types of analogies, covering all content areas:

- Synonyms—Mother : Mom::Father : Dad

- Antonyms—Inhale : Exhale::Stop : Go

- Definition—Box : Container constructed with four sides::Ball : A spherical object

- Object to function—Pen : Write::Car : Drive

- Part to whole—Tongue : Mouth::Head : Body

- Type or example—Flu : Illness::Volvo : Car

- Location—Paris : France::Book : Library

- Components—Cake : Batter::Computer : Chips

Research suggests that children's ability to use analogies is related to their working memory capacity. What is very exciting about this research is that very young children can learn information using analogies (Singer-Freeman, 2003).

Metaphoric teaching can help students identify what they do not understand. Metaphors and analogies emphasize relationships and help students recognize and understand patterns. Idioms and similes can also help students organize and connect information (Richards, 2003).

Explaining

Cause and effect are elements of this understanding. Upon being given a description of a system, a student develops and uses a cause-and-effect model. The student must understand the specifics of the system and the relationships they have to one another.

Cause-and-effect relationships can be expressed in an if-then statement; for example:

- If you are exposed to a flu virus, then you may get the flu.
- If you talk on your cell phone while driving, then you may have an accident.

Your students may use words that connect the cause and effect, such as *influence*, *changes*, *why*, *cause*, *effect*, *as a result*, *because of*, *the reason for*, *consequence*, and *decrease*.

Students are naturally curious and want to know why things happen. They can set up their recoding by starting with the effect and then the cause or by starting with the cause:

- Peter is angry with Michael. Michael told Peter a lie.
- Michael told Peter a lie, so Peter is angry.

Much of the content that we teach involves cause-and-effect principles. Nothing happens without a reason. We often ask questions that refer to a cause-and-effect relationship without using the words:

- What happens when you pour lemon juice into a glass of milk?
- What happens if you make noise in a library?
- Why is it important to drive carefully?
- What happens if you eat too much?

A T chart may be used as a graphic organizer for cause and effect (see Appendix B). If there are more causes or more effects, several options are possible.

Mental Note: Students create their own memories when they recode new material.

Recoding Using Nonlinguistic Representations

Nonlinguistic representations are any form of information that does not rely on words, such as kinesthetic activity, drawn pictures, and graphic representations.

Basically, the student takes semantic information and makes it nonsemantic in nature.

Many researchers believe that we always store information in both language and images. For instance, Marzano, Pickering, and Pollack (2001) used several types of graphic organizers as part of the examples for interpreting, exemplifying, classifying, summarizing, inferring, comparing, and explaining. Results of their research showed a percentile gain in student achievement of up to 40 percent.

Some students may opt to recode by drawing pictures, creating models, or moving. Using the T chart is useful for this approach. On the left side, students show semantically what they know or understand; on the right side, they draw a picture or symbol.

Mind mapping is a brain-compatible note-taking strategy that was developed by Tony Buzan (1974) in England and has been especially effective for students with dyslexia. Because students with dyslexia have some interference in their brains with the language center, they found great success using only pictures and symbols for their mind maps (Kenyon, 2002).

Keep in mind that once your students have recoded nonlinguistically, they should try to recode using words. Because recoding assists in conceptual understanding, once a concept is understood, transferring to the semantic pathway offers beneficial practice for assessment purposes.

Recoding Procedural Knowledge

The purpose of recoding is ascertaining whether the student understands. This holds true for procedural knowledge. Say you've introduced a procedure and your students have had some time to reflect. Now you want them to recode the procedure—put it in their own terms to be sure that they understand the concepts behind it. For instance, if you use the following procedure to solve story problems in math, you may want your students to rewrite the steps in their own words:

1. What is the question?
2. What are the important facts?
3. Do you have enough information to solve the problem?
4. Do you have too much information?

5. What operation will you use?

6. Label your answer.

7. Is your answer reasonable?

Then perhaps they could apply a problem to the procedure to see how it works. If their recoded steps don't solve the problem, they may want to make some changes. This approach may work for science and other content area procedures as well.

Decision making is another procedure that we encourage students to master. Students may use a framework like the following to guide them:

1. Define a problem.

2. Establish goals/objectives.

3. Define criteria for selection.

4. Gather relevant information.

5. Identify feasible alternatives.

6. Predict future consequences.

7. Compare alternatives.

8. Select the best alternative.

Crannell (1994) states, "Professional mathematicians spend most of their time writing: communicating with colleagues, applying for grants, publishing papers, writing memos and syllabi. Writing well is extremely important to mathematicians, since poor writers have a hard time getting published, getting attention from the deans, and obtaining funding. It is ironic but true that most mathematicians spend more time writing than they spend doing math." She suggests that the following steps be applied to mathematical writing:

1. Clearly restate the problem to be solved.

2. State the answer in a complete sentence that stands on its own.

3. Clearly state the assumptions that underlie the formulas.

4. Provide a paragraph that explains how the problem will be approached.

5. Clearly label diagrams, tables, graphs, or other visual representations of the math (if these are indeed used).

6. Define all variables used.

7. Explain how each formula is derived, or where it can be found.

8. Give acknowledgment where it is due.

9. In this paper, are the spelling, grammar, and punctuation correct?

10. In this paper, is the mathematics correct?

11. In this paper, did the writer solve the question that was originally asked?

For more information about math, see ASCD's (2001) *The Brain and Math* video series.

Writing across the curriculum is an important component to creating good writers. Research strongly supports the fact that students reinforce their learning when they write about their content, be it concepts, facts, or procedures. In *Writing Across the Curriculum*, Cooke (1991) states, "When we ask our students to write . . . we are encouraging them to engage actively with the subject matter in our disciplines: to see patterns, connect ideas, make meanings—in other words, to learn" (p. 5).

Mental Note: Students must understand the concepts underlying the procedures they learn to make the information transferable.

Manipulating Information in Working Memory

The process of recoding gives the brain time and opportunity to start making connections. When students can state facts, concepts, and procedures in their own words, ownership of the material begins.

Recoding needs to take place in the classroom. Sending students home with new material to recode may be stressful. This is not the time for homework and practice; rather, this is the time to ask questions and iron out wrinkles in thinking. At this point in the seven-step process, students have just gone through a reflective period and are "trying out" the material. This opportunity to manipulate new knowledge in working memory is the beginning of setting up neural connections in the brain that, if accurate, will be rehearsed to become lasting long-term memories.

Reflection

1. Consider your current practice. Is recoding always a process you include? How can you incorporate it into your lessons?

2. Regularly following these steps will help students evaluate what strategies are most helpful and make the most sense to them. Examine what recoding practices you have been using. Are you more comfortable with some than others? Step out of your comfort zone, and introduce your students to as many of these research-based strategies as you can, so they have the opportunity to apply them in many situations.

3. Remember learning styles. The visual learner needs to write information and see it. The auditory learner may need to hear it first. The kinesthetic learner may need to build a model. How do learning styles fit into your lesson plans?

Reinforce

Feedback is vital to learning.

One of the most effective means to cultivate a goal-oriented culture
is to regularly reinforce and recognize improvement efforts,
both privately and publicly.

—*Mike Schmoker*, Results: The Key to Continuous School Improvement

I am observing a prekindergarten classroom as part of my job for the state board of edu-
cation. Although I started my teaching career at this level, it has been many years since I
worked with this age group. The teacher, Mrs. Keene, is playing a familiar game with
them that I remember from my childhood: "Hot and Cold." One child is "it" and is asked
to leave the room. The class chooses an object. When the child returns, the class sings a
song, getting louder when the child is "hot," or close to the object, or singing softly when
the child is "cold," or far from the object.

As I watch the class, I think of the possible purposes of the game. Certainly the chil-
dren must be making decisions about when to get louder or softer. Self-control is chal-
lenged as the little ones want to point or give other clues as to the selected article. What I
find particularly interesting is the feedback that the singing provides. This reinforcement is
offered continually. The children do not get frustrated as they search for the target.
Through the continuous feedback, every child is successful.

Mrs. Keene changes the game on my second visit. This time an object is chosen, a red Lego block, and is hidden when the student who is "it" leaves the room. Upon returning, the students take turns saying either "hot" or "cold" depending on how close "it" is to the object. Again, all are successful.

Then an interesting turn of events occurs. A child from the kindergarten class walks into the room to give Mrs. Keene a note. He had been in Mrs. Keene's class last year and remembered the game. He announces, "I'm going to play, too. Tell me when I'm hot or cold or getting warmer." The students comply. But there is a problem. This boy was not present when the object was picked, so no matter how "hot" he gets, he must randomly guess at what object is the right one. His frustration is evident, and he quits before he can choose the red Lego block. After he leaves the room, one of the children, Sally, asks why he didn't pick the Lego block. She is concerned that her participation was somehow faulty. But the problem was not the feedback. In fact, the feedback was perfect. But the effectiveness of feedback relies on the student knowing what the target is.

Mrs. Keene takes time to explain to her class why the game didn't work for her former student. She gives examples of how goals and targets help us accomplish what we are after.

Reinforcement, the act of encouraging and strengthening, is dependent on clear goals and targets. Once our students have recoded the material to help them with their conceptual and procedural understandings, it is time for feedback.

What Is Reinforcing?

Reinforcing is providing a verbal or symbolic reward for academic performance or effort (Northwest Regional Educational Laboratory [NWREL], 2002). Feedback as reinforcement offers encouragement and the opportunity to fortify what the students understand. We can let our students know whether their perceptions and understanding are correct, and, if necessary, we can reshape or reteach. Feedback also allows students to change their conceptual understandings before they rehearse for long-term memory. We want to be able to ascertain whether our students get it. Once we know that they comprehend, we want to strengthen that understanding and start the process of permanent storage. This is not time for a grade. This is only the launching of their learning. Reinforcement provides time in working memory to make necessary changes. In other words, information must be "perfect" before it enters permanent storage. Does instructional reinforcement raise student achievement? Teachers who routinely provide feedback and reinforcement regarding student learning improve results. The reinforcement step is always dependent on an academic goal. These teachers make use of peer evaluation techniques, provide computer-assisted instructional activities that give students immediate feedback regarding their learning performance, assign homework that is corrected and returned promptly—either in class by the students or later by the teacher—and use peer tutoring strategies that include training students to provide each other feedback and reinforcement (NWREL, 2002).

Mental Note: Feedback is more effective when it is presented as a method of improvement.

According to Hattie (1999), "The simplest prescription for improving education must be 'dollops of feedback'—providing information how and why the child understands and misunderstands, and what directions the student must take to improve." His analysis of more than 8,000 studies shows clearly that feedback enhances student achievement more than any other strategy.

Types of Feedback

Feedback comes in many structures and from many different sources. Students receive feedback from the teacher, classmates, and even themselves. Grades are a form of feedback, yet at this step in the memory process, the student is not ready to be graded. In fact, it is still too soon for homework, but this *is* time for assessment.

Chappuis and Stiggins (2002) speak of two kinds of assessment: assessment *of* learning and assessment *for* learning. Assessment for learning includes a continual effort to provide feedback in every part of the teaching situation. Just as reflection is needed every step of the way for long-term retention, reinforcement is also necessary. To improve memory, feedback increases interest to keep students on task, and it allows for adjustments. When 1st grade students were taught a rehearsal strategy to help them remember material, only those who received feedback on how well it worked continued to use it (Higbee, 1996).

In *Balanced Assessment: The Key to Accountability and Improved Student Learning*, the National Education Association (2003) notes that achievement gains are maximized in contexts where educators increase the accuracy of classroom assessments; provide students with frequent informative feedback (versus infrequent or merely judgmental feedback); and involve students deeply in the classroom assessment, record keeping, and communication processes.

At this important step on the road to long-term retention and transfer, we can look at Stronge's (2002) conclusions in regard to ongoing assessment and feedback from effective teachers. Stronge came to the following conclusions about effective teachers:

- They use pre-assessments to support targeted teaching of skills.

- They implement good monitoring strategies by directing questions to the lesson's targets.

- They think through likely misconceptions that students may have and monitor them to look for those misconceptions.

- They give clear, specific, and timely feedback throughout the teaching/learning process.

- They give feedback in a supportive and encouraging manner.

- They reteach material to students who did not achieve mastery.

Connellan (2003) describes three types of feedback: *motivational* feedback to accelerate improvement, *informational* feedback that gives students a way to measure progress, and *developmental* feedback to help those students who are not performing. Each of these types of feedback is useful in the classroom and helps with reinforcement. We need to value all forms of feedback and possibly use them all together.

> **Mental Note: Feedback provides the reinforcement students need to remain motivated.**

Motivational Feedback

Motivational feedback can be divided into three distinct forms: positive feedback, negative feedback, and what Connellan (2003) calls "extinction." *Positive* feedback is reinforcing. *Negative* feedback, if given incorrectly, is punishing. *Extinction* is the result of receiving no feedback at all. This is the least motivating response that can be offered.

Goleman (1998) refers to a study of MBA students and the effects of feedback. Some students received feedback that was positive, some negative, and others no feedback at all. The students were told that their work would be compared to hundreds of others who had performed the same creative problem-solving task. Those who received no feedback suffered the same loss of self-confidence as those who were criticized. It appears that depriving students of feedback can inhibit their future performance.

Keep in mind that the purpose of motivational feedback is to cheer students on, to help them do their best and enjoy peak performance. This experience includes challenges that offer high energy, extreme effort, and positive feelings, including those that come from positive feedback. During such a surge of "good" stress, adrenaline, norepinephrine, and serotonin are released to move us toward our goals. The more negative stress and sense of threat that may result from negative and extinctive feedback, however, are operated by a different system in the brain that releases vast amounts of the stress hormone cortisol, as well as an excess of other neurotransmitters. This chemical overload interrupts our thinking by taking over working memory (Goleman, 1998). Ideally, then, we want to seize opportunities to provide our students with positive feedback and thereby enhance their memory skills and, ultimately, their learning.

Mental Note: There are three types of motivational feedback.

Positive Feedback

Positive feedback is the reinforcement that makes students want to keep doing what they've been doing. Connellan (2003) offers five principles of positive feedback:

- Reinforce immediately.
- Reinforce any improvement, not only excellence.
- Be specific in your reinforcement.
- Continuously reinforce new behaviors.
- Reinforce good habits intermittently.

Immediate feedback, the first principle, does not have to be instantaneous. That is, it may sometimes take you a little time to check a student's recoded material. After all, feedback is a form of assessment that is formative, and it brings students into the assessment process. You are building a framework for further learning and understanding of concepts. If you have the ability to cruise the room as students recode material, you may be able to offer feedback verbally. Keep in mind, too, that your kinesthetic students may respond more to a pat on the back, your auditory students to verbal encouragement, and the visuals to a smile, a nod, or a mark on their papers.

The second principle—to reinforce any improvement—is one that we teachers need to consider. In our fast-paced educational environment where we constantly fight for time, it is easy to overlook the baby steps that some students take toward understanding. We are programmed to look for bottom lines and have been trained to seek and admire excellence. The truth is that some students may only be scratching the surface in their recoding efforts. To assist our students on their journey to long-term memory, we must let them acquire awareness in bits and pieces. Any improvement we detect, then, is worthy of our positive feedback.

Specificity, the third principle of positive feedback, is also sometimes difficult for teachers. We often are very general with our positive comments: "Good description" or "Nice comparisons." When it comes to finding faults, however, we can be very specific. We may start by expressing something generally good, and then become picky about what is wrong. An example might be, "I like the graphic organizer you chose for this concept, but a Venn diagram can't be used this way. You can't put contrasting information in the middle, and you are wasting space by writing the similarities twice in the outside areas." I am not saying that remaining positive *and* specific is not a difficult task with some students; in fact, it can seem almost impossible at times. Keep in mind, however, that if a student has attempted to do the work, then something positive is indeed happening. An approach might be, "I can tell that you are really trying to gain an understanding of this concept. Let's look at what you have here. Your mind map may need some revision. Your first major detail needs more support. Your second and third details have interesting symbols, and you might want to add a few key words or phrases here. The last detail is your best; it is very clear that you understand this part."

The fourth principle of positive feedback reminds us to reinforce new behaviors. New behaviors may include using new types of organizers, new approaches to recoding, or improvement in any skills. Because these are new, they must be reinforced continuously. When these actions become second nature to the students, you can shift from continuous reinforcement to intermittent support, the basis of the last principle. At this point, the students may even be able to reinforce themselves. This is a time for metacognition—thinking about how they are thinking—and giving themselves positive feedback for their accomplishments.

Mental Note: Give positive feedback to students who are making small gains.

Negative Feedback

How do we handle the student who isn't meeting the expectations on the recoded material? Colbert and Knapp (2000) suggest the following steps:

1. Focus the evaluation.

2. Point out the original goals.

3. Identify responsibility.

4. Communicate specific components.

5. Discuss a new plan of action.

6. Confirm correct results.

Let's explore an example of these steps in action:

As the students identify similarities and differences of Civil War generals, Mrs. Ling circulates and peruses her students' Venn diagrams. When she reaches Carmen's desk, she sees that Carmen's recoded material is a paragraph.

Mrs. Ling asks, "Carmen, are you going to create your graphic organizer from the paragraph?" (Focus.)

"I like to write in sentences," Carmen responds.

"The instructions are to create a Venn diagram showing the similarities in the overlapping areas of the circles and the differences in the outer areas. (Point out original goals.) *Look at the one on the overhead," Mrs. Ling suggests. "Your job is to show me that you can use a Venn properly.* (Identify responsibility.) *Do you understand that you must include characteristics of the generals that are alike and those that are different?* (Communicate specific components.) *Below your paragraph draw the graphic organizer.* (Discuss the plan of action.) *That's right. Fill it in with some of that information from your paragraph and I'll come back to check on you."* (Confirm results.)

Another way to keep away from negative feedback is to guide the student to the proper understanding through Socratic dialogue. Socratic dialogue involves several categories of questions: clarification questions, questions about the initial question or issue, assumption probes, reason and evidence probes, origin or source questions, implication and consequence probes, and viewpoint questions. Sample questions from Paul's (1993) work are provided in Figure 4.1.

Figure 4.1

Socratic Questions Adapted from the Work of Richard Paul (1993)

Type of Question	Examples
Clarification Questions	• What do you mean by ...? • What is your main point? • How does _____ relate to_____? • Could you put that another way? • Can you give me an example?
Questions about the Question	• How can we find out? • Is the question clear? • Why is this question important? • To answer this question, what would we have to answer first?
Assumption Probes	• What are you assuming? • What could we assume instead? • Why would someone make this assumption?
Reason and Evidence Probes	• What would be an example? • How do you know? • What led you to that belief? • What would change your mind? • How does that apply to this case?
Origin or Source Questions	• Where did you get this idea? • Have you always felt this way? • What effect would that have? • What is an alternative?
Implication and Consequence Probes	• If this is true, what else should also be true? • What would be the effect?
Viewpoint Questions	• How would other groups respond? • Why have you chosen this perspective? • What would someone who disagrees say?

Socratic questioning and dialogue allows us to lead the student to his own destination. The questions keep the student on track to develop a conceptual understanding of the material. The questioning strategies may build upon each other, or they may simply lead the teacher and student on a more random journey that ends with a positive outcome. So, rather than telling a student that his understanding is somehow faulty, the student is given the opportunity to change his thinking and recode the material in a more satisfying manner.

Having a Socratic dialogue with students helps them explore the depth and breadth of their understanding. When I started using this method with students in the 1980s, I found it challenging at first. But students began to thank me for sticking with them and helping them come to terms with their understanding.

The students have just finished recoding their new material on a short story by Shirley Jackson, The Lottery. *The unit thus far has consisted of the following:*

Reach: When the students entered the room, Ms. Brown was folding small white pieces of paper and placing them in a box. When they were seated, she began. "Class, I ordered tickets to the play based on the story we are about to read, The Lottery. *There are 27 students in the class, so I asked for 28 tickets to include me. Unfortunately, they mailed only 27 tickets. When I called, they said the play was completely sold out. So, to be fair about this, I have put 27 blank pieces of paper in this box. I also put one piece in it that is marked with an x. We will all take turns drawing from the box. The person who gets the x will be unable to go to the theater with us and will instead go to another English class." The students were curious about the process. Everyone drew. They were told they could not open their papers until every person had drawn. Together they opened their papers.*

John W. received the x. Some of the students snickered. Many breathed a sigh of relief. No one questioned the teacher's authority to have a lottery. John said it wasn't fair. He didn't deserve to be left out. After all, he was a good student. Someone who doesn't work hard should be left out.

Reflect: After revealing that, indeed, there were 28 tickets, the students were then put into groups for a four-corner reflection. The teacher posted a question in each corner of the room, with space on the paper to write ideas. The four questions were as follows:

1. How do you feel about this lottery?

2. How could this decision have been made fairly?

3. How do your peers influence your decision making?

4. Why were you willing to leave one person out?

The students went from corner to corner discussing each question and adding comments to the sheets.

Recode: The students were then asked to read The Lottery. Their recoding assignment was to exemplify. They were to list the pros and cons of following traditions and rituals.

Reinforce: In small-group discussions, students shared their lists. Ms. Brown circulated to offer feedback. At one table, Jess and Robert were arguing.

"You're nuts," Robert said. "Birthday parties are not rituals."

"What do you mean by ritual?" Ms. Brown asked.

"Rituals are things you do over and over," Robert replied.

"Can you give me an example?" she inquired.

"Yeah, like going to church."

"What elements of church make it a ritual?"

"You know, you go and they do the same stuff all the time. The service follows the same pages in the book. The people sing the same hymns. They go every Sunday. That's a ritual," Robert declared.

"What are you assuming about birthday parties?"

"Birthday parties are different every time. You can go to a movie or have a big party or do nothing," he replied.

"What is Jess saying to you that you don't agree with?" she probed.

"Jess says that birthdays are rituals because you are celebrating the day you were born each year, and that you have cake and ice cream, and you get cards."

"How do birthdays once a year relate to going to church, Robert?"

He thought for several moments. The teacher gave him the wait time even though others in his group had their hands up and wanted to answer.

Robert said, "I think I can see it now. Once a year or once a week, the same basic concept is being replayed. OK, I think I understand ritual better now."

The Socratic questioning technique allowed Robert to come to his own conclusions. Ms. Brown provided the feedback that would change his understanding of the concept and give him a greater chance of storing correct information.

Extinction?

My son Josh walks in after school and quietly puts his books down. His sister Marnie is doing her homework, and I am doing mine.

"So, how was your day?" I ask, as I look up from grading papers.

"Oh, you can see me?" he asks.

Somewhat startled, I put my pen down. "Of course, I can see you. What kind of question is that?"

"I thought maybe I was invisible," Josh replies.

Thoughts of insanity and drug abuse pass through my mind. "Please explain yourself," I ask.

"We had to turn in the outlines for our projects in chemistry," Josh begins. "Mrs. Green walked from table to table and picked up the papers. Gina and Sarah's was first. She looked it over and got a big grin on her face. She said, 'Girls, I think you've got it!' Gina and Sarah were all excited. Then she went to Justin and Jason's table and picked up their outline. She looked at it and got a puzzled look on her face. She said something like, 'Are you sure you two understand what an outline is supposed to look like?' Boy, were they embarrassed. She came to my table next. She picked up our outline, looked at it, and didn't say a word. I couldn't even see an expression on her face. It was like Dan and I didn't even exist."

"How did she react to the other kids' papers?" I inquire.

"I don't know. She looked at a few, and then the bell rang. Everyone had to turn the papers in quickly," he replies.

"At least she didn't say anything negative about yours," Marnie notes.

"Are you kidding?" Josh barks. "Negative would have been better than nothing!"

"Well, I'm sure she'll give you some feedback," I suggest optimistically.

"You don't get it, Mom—she did give me feedback! She told me my work didn't matter!"

That conversation taught me a lesson. I started thinking about the way I respond to my students. How many times have I made some of them feel invisible? I remembered what my principal said to me: "My job is to bring out the best in people. That's your job, too." Mrs. Green certainly wasn't bringing out the best in Josh, but I bet she was like me and didn't have a clue what she had done.

My children happened to have the same English teacher in high school. We still make jokes about the papers that she never handed back. It can be funny now, years later, but it wasn't funny to her students back then. They would work very hard on papers and never get any type of feedback. Let's give her the benefit of the doubt. She had between 100 and 150 students each day. That's a lot of papers to grade. But she didn't have to grade every one of them. It is OK to assign work and not grade it, but someone must comment upon it. Always give feedback on the recoding that you say you are going to give feedback on.

Students can assess themselves and assess each other. If you are having students share their initial recoding, working in cooperative groups may be timely and helpful. A sharing of the recoded material followed by a discussion may clarify many cloudy areas. This approach will also give you time to cruise the room and listen to each group. You may then want to collect this first attempt at the material for a quick perusal for the next day. These results will give you the information you need to decide whether to add more material, reteach, or move on to the rehearsal stage. A rubric like that in Figure 4.2 may be helpful for you and your students.

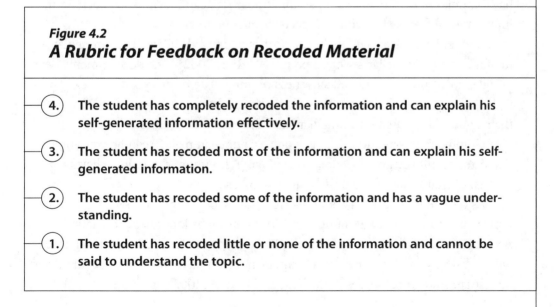

Figure 4.2
A Rubric for Feedback on Recoded Material

4. The student has completely recoded the information and can explain his self-generated information effectively.

3. The student has recoded most of the information and can explain his self-generated information.

2. The student has recoded some of the information and has a vague understanding.

1. The student has recoded little or none of the information and cannot be said to understand the topic.

Mental Note: Students benefit from providing feedback to other students.

Informational Feedback

Whereas motivational feedback acts to hasten improvement, informational feedback offers students a visual representation of progress. Connellan (2003) makes three points about informational feedback:

- It should be goal oriented.
- It should be immediate.
- It should be graphic.

The chapter-opening scenario of the prekindergarten class's game of Hot or Cold made it apparent that the target must be obvious—the premise of Connellan's first point. Gone are the days of keeping goals and objectives from students. If you are teaching students writing strategies that emphasize organization, they should have samples of quality essays illustrating those strategies. With such background, informational feedback becomes especially valuable.

A meta-analysis of reinforcement studies addressed the need for immediate reinforcement, Connellan's second point (NWREL, 2002). The developmental level of the student predicted the effectiveness of immediate or delayed feedback. That is, for younger children, immediate feedback was best, but for the older students, the response was equal for immediate and delayed reinforcement.

Graphic representations, the last point Connellan makes, can be very influential forms of informational feedback (see Figure 4.3 for an example). Charts, graphs, diagrams, and simple symbols may be useful.

As a teacher concerned about learning styles, one might think that a graphic representation may not be as important for auditory or kinesthetic learners. According to a meta-analysis (Marzano, Pickering, & Pollack, 2001) the feedback with the strongest effect involves an explanation, verbal or written, of accurate and inaccurate student responses. Crossland and Clarke (2002) firmly promote the use

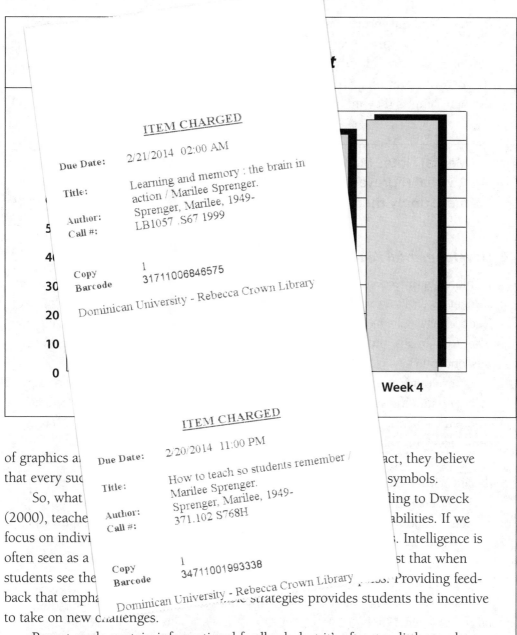

Week 4

of graphics a[...] [...]act, they believe
that every suc[...] [...]symbols.

So, what [...] [...]ling to Dweck
(2000), teache[...] [...]abilities. If we
focus on indivi[...] [...]. Intelligence is
often seen as a [...] [...]st that when
students see the [...] [...]. Providing feedback that empha[...] [...]ic strategies provides students the incentive
to take on new challenges.

Report cards contain informational feedback, but it's often too little, too late.
Portfolios are one way of bringing curriculum, instruction, and assessment

together. Without formal grades, a portfolio may contain informational feedback from the teacher, from peers, and from the student herself as a reflection. Working portfolios are nontraditional and brain-compatible forms of assessment that may show growth over time. The application of concepts may be easier to observe through samples that are included in a portfolio (Sprenger, 1999).

Mental Note: Many parents desire informational feedback. A visual representation other than the traditional report card may supply them with the knowledge they need.

Developmental Feedback

Reinforcement feedback is assessment *for* learning when either the teacher or the student uses that information to inform teaching and to influence learning. This feedback is *developmental* when you affect the student's performance behavior. You want to influence the conceptual understanding before it becomes a permanent misconception.

Developmental feedback includes first a statement of the problem and then some questioning strategies. You want to be sure to provide this sort of feedback before the student experiences a sense of helplessness. In the study of *The Lottery*, some developmental feedback might begin like this:

"Sabrina, I see that you are using a T chart. I don't see examples of rituals and traditions. You seem to have characteristics instead."

"I just don't get this. That story was kind of hard to read," Sabrina responds.

At this point, try to help the student correct the error or misconception:

"What can you do to adjust this?" No accusations. No blame.

Sabrina replies, *"I guess I can't think of any examples."*

"Let's take a look at the characteristics you have written down."

Sabrina checks her chart and says, *"Traditions are things that people do because other people did them before."*

"Can you think of another word for that?"

"No."

"Who are the people that were before you?"

"You mean, like my parents and grandparents?" she asks.

"Yes. Did they do anything that you now do?"

"No," is her reply.

"Does your mom do anything that your grandma did?"

"My mom says it's a custom to hang mistletoe above the front door at Christmas, so you have to kiss everyone who comes in! That is so gross."

"So, is a custom the same thing as tradition?"

Sabrina thinks. "I guess so."

Now is the time to reinforce:

"Custom is a synonym for tradition. Can you think of another custom?"

"Well, it's customary in this country to put your hand over your heart when you say the Pledge of Allegiance."

"I think you have the idea now. That's another example. See if you can think of more. I'll be back to check on you."

The process described here consisted of five steps:

1. Describe the problem.

2. Invite solutions.

3. Look at options.

4. Call attention to constructive responses.

5. Arrange for further feedback.

Sabrina felt helpless in this situation. She was resistant, because she doubted her abilities. Although she tried to blame the story for being too difficult, the teacher could not let her use that opinion as an excuse. After all, examples of traditions can be constructed without having read the story. The recoding strategy was used to teach the concept of exemplifying, the meaning of tradition and ritual, and the ability to identify similarities and differences. The teacher is attempting to assist Sabrina in her understanding of these through some reinforcement strategies.

Mental Note: Differentiation is key when providing developmental feedback. Students who require this type of reinforcement may have missed something in the original instruction.

Feedback Results

Our brains want us to be safe and happy; survival is at the forefront of all that we do. Feedback offers the opportunity to fulfill those needs. The emotional systems for both fear and pleasure are involved as working memory manipulates information and asks for reinforcement.

Through understanding, our students can be successful and feel in control. Emotional areas of the brain are involved in learning situations that include feedback (Zull, 2002). Many memory researchers agree that emotional involvement creates stronger memories (Gordon & Berger, 2003).

Studies show that providing feedback increases student achievement. According to work by Marzano (1998), for example, a 29-percentile point difference in student learning can be achieved through frequent feedback.

The type of feedback received also makes a difference in its effectiveness. Butler (1987) studied the effect of different types of feedback on students after an assessment. Some received written comments addressing specific targets that the students were aware of before the assessment (developmental feedback), some received grades alone (informational feedback), and some received grades and comments (a combination of the two). Interestingly, when these students performed two more tasks, those who received comments alone increased significantly. Those who received grades alone declined on the second task, but picked up on the third. The students who received comments and grades declined on the subsequent tasks.

Reflection

1. Feedback should be timely. Some consultants (e.g., Tileston, 2004) suggest that feedback should be given every 30 minutes. Examine your feedback strategies. What kind of reinforcement could you add?

2. Keep learning styles in mind in relation to reinforcement. Different learners may require different forms of feedback. For instance, a kinesthetic learner may literally need a pat on the back. Or take a walk with this learner as you provide informational feedback.

3. Reinforcement must be specific. This is the time for students to "get it right." Before you send them on to the next step, you want to be sure that homework and practice are possible with their current understanding.

Rehearse

To get information into long-term memory, it must be rehearsed.

> We remember better the more fully we process new subject matter.
>
> —*Larry Squire and Eric Kandel,* Memory: From Mind to Molecules

I run across the hall to the 8th grade history teacher's room. I want to borrow her globe for a lesson I am going to begin when my students finish writing in their journals. She is in the midst of doing a KWL chart with her class. I stand outside the door for a moment to observe these students whom I had last year.

"What do you know about democracy?" she begins. "Let's brainstorm what we know or think we know and write it in the column under K." She pauses to give her students some wait time.

There is silence. She glances at the clock and watches as the second hand goes a full 10 seconds. There are still no responses.

"So, are you telling me that you know nothing about democracy? How about a definition? Can anyone tell me what democracy is?"

Again. Silence.

I am ready to freak out! These were my students last year. We studied the democratic system. Inside my head I am yelling, "People! Government by the people! Don't you remember? Were you not in my room last year? Did you not take and pass a test on this information? What is wrong with you? . . . Or am I a horrible teacher?"

I enter the room at this point to retrieve the globe. I am hoping that my interruption will not increase thoughts of my incompetence in the teacher's mind. As I walk to her [desk, I notice some of the students staring at me]. Their gaze continues as I stop, ask for [...] eral of the students who were looking [...] Oh, I remember about democracy. We [...] room!"

[...st]udents enter our classes at the begin-[ning...kn]ow what was covered the previous [...] remember. In most cases, they did [...s]ome of the information from long-term [...] classroom, a number of the students [...usin]g their memory banks for information [...fro]m me. These experiences were recorded [...no]t yet "transferred" to the semantic path-[way...] without my presence. I was the connec-[tion...]

[...al]l, our students may do well on a class-[...s]hortly thereafter. The fact is that you [...the]y learned. In addition, my students [...sp]ecific cue. Information must be stored [...] accessible without cues. For some stu-dents, this so-called transfer rate can take a very long time (Siegel, 1999).

Step 5 takes us to the rehearsal process. It is this step that promotes the storage of information in long-term memory. Many variables interact in preparing information in ways that will make it accessible and transferable. Keep in mind that whenever we have given our students the opportunity to reflect, they have had *some* rehearsal time. Thinking about what they have learned causes them to repeat the information verbally or mentally in their own words.

In this chapter, we will look at the importance of rote and elaborate rehearsal, multiple memory pathways, homework and practice, and the necessity of sleep. I will incorporate higher levels of thinking into the rehearsal process as well. A report authored by Harold Wenglinsky (2002) of the Educational Testing Service concludes that students of teachers who emphasize higher-order thinking skills in math and hands-on learning activities in science outperform their peers considerably. Using the scientifically based strategies introduced in the recoding stage will also assist students in remembering and raising achievement.

What Is Rehearsal?

Glenn is making me crazy. This child is an auditory learner, and he loves music more than anything else in the world. He is constantly tapping out a beat on his desk or his book. For an 11-year-old, he knows more lyrics than any person I know.

It is Tuesday morning, and we are just finishing math. Our next subject to tackle is science. I have recently introduced new vocabulary. The students were to create a visual or some other mnemonic device to help them remember. As I am trying to determine the best way to share our pictures, I am interrupted by Glenn's tapping . . . again. I watch as he mouths some rap and taps on his desk. Other students are also observing. Some are nodding their heads to the beat. Some of the girls look at Glenn as though he is a rap star. I think, "Just what every 5th grader needs—groupies!"

I am at the end of my rope. "Glenn, what are you doing?"

"I'm practicing, Mrs. Sprenger," he replies.

"Well, we're not working on a rap concert for you today," I counter. "We have important vocabulary to cover."

"But that's what I'm doing," he says defensively. "I'm rapping my vocabulary so I can remember it." He proceeds to share his rap on the parts of the heart. It actually is quite good. Several of the students want to learn it. They think it is the best mnemonic they have ever heard.

You've probably seen the commercial on television. A young man is driving down the street, his head bobbing and his lips moving. Young women see him and are smitten by what seems to be his musical sense; he appears to be "cool." He continues his drive until we, the audience, are finally allowed inside the car to hear what we believe will be a song. Instead, we hear him repeating over and over again to a rhythm . . . his grocery list!

Information that enters immediate memory is lost rapidly unless it is manipulated in some way. Rehearsal, a form of such mental manipulation, comes in two types: rote and elaborative. *Rote* rehearsal is effective when the information will be used in the same format or design as the rehearsal (Marzano, 1992). Multiplication facts, states and capitals, and the order of the presidents are examples of material that can be rehearsed in a rote fashion. *Elaborative* rehearsal is more useful in our classrooms as we teach semantic information because it relies on creating meaning, and meaningful information is more memorable. In other words, elaborative rehearsal allows the student to make connections to information that may already be stored (Tileston, 2004).

According to Marzano, Pickering, and Pollack (2001), skill learning requires at least 24 practices to reach 80 percent proficiency. The Power Law of Learning (Anderson, 2000), which explains how long it takes to recognize accurately information that has been presented, suggests that it takes many exposures to information for accurate memory. Each time information is offered, the number of seconds before it is recognized decreases.

Noted researcher Howard Eichenbaum (2003) refers to the premise that our semantic memories are born out of our episodic memories. We live our lives in episodes. As we derive information from each episode, the information is stored in the brain. The brain takes the repeated bits of information out of the experiences, and those become our semantic memories. An example would be all of the attributes we know about dogs. The fact that dogs wag their tails may have come from several "dog" experiences where we saw this take place. We have heard dogs barking many times, so we may associate this trait with dogs. The experiences themselves may have escaped our memories so that we no longer know the time and the place that these events occurred, but the distinguishing characteristics of the animals stay with us due to the repetition of those features. As this theory is generally accepted, providing numerous episodes for our students is an example and a necessary component of elaborative rehearsal.

The opening scenario in which the students could not retrieve information on democracy until I entered the room also validates this theory. The students will reactivate whatever networks of neurons may have been created in previous episodes on the topic. Until the memories are consolidated in the brain, they must be retrieved via the pathway where they were stored. Memories are also sensitive to disruption until they are consolidated. Eventually, the information will become accessible without any specific triggers or cues.

 Mental Note: Memories must be rehearsed in multiple ways to store them in many areas of the brain.

Why Rehearse?

To *rehearse* is to recite or repeat in private for experiment and improvement. Students must try out their newfound learning. Through the first four steps, we have set up a network of brain connections. Through the recoding and reinforcement steps, that network is accurate or has been corrected. To help my students understand the idea that concepts and skills must be practiced, I use the following activity.

This exercise works best in a large room; I use the library, cafeteria, or gymnasium or take the students outside if the weather is conducive. I divide the students into two groups, spreading them out, and give the student closest to the front in each group a beach ball. This person is the "sender." I designate the person in each group who is farthest away as the "receiver." The rules are simple: The beach ball must get to the receiver without the students moving their feet and without the ball touching the ground. Beach balls are so light that most students cannot throw them directly to the target easily. Therefore, the groups must figure a way to get the ball to the receiver. Through trial and error, the students finally figure out what order of tossing the ball to people on the team will work to get the ball to its destination. There may be some applause when the teams accomplish their task. But now, I look at my watch and say, "Well, both groups got the job done, but that took a long time. Let's try it again!" With a little competition and the clock ticking, the students try to relay the ball faster. In some cases, they use fewer people to intercept. Sometimes the tosses go wild and the ball drops. Then they must start over. Eventually, each team figures out how to get the ball to the receiver quickly. They believe they have triumphed at that point.

I take time to discuss what happened. The students all had to work together. They had to figure out which combination worked best. But had they really learned? In order for the learning to become permanent, they would have to practice this routine over and over. Then tomorrow or next week we could reassemble, and everyone would remember where they stood and to whom the ball should be tossed. This memory creation to enhance performance underscores the importance of rehearsal. Students who are athletes comment about the continual practices with their teams. They come to the realization that practice is setting up networks in their brains.

This activity makes an important point about learning and memory. Learning something—that is, getting to the "aha" moment—isn't enough for attaining memory and transfer. Rehearsal of that enlightenment accounts for some of the difference between walking into a classroom at the beginning of the school year with the ability to access prior learning and not having that capability.

In *Classroom Instruction That Works* (Marzano, Pickering, & Pollack, 2001) studies are cited (Ross, 1988; Bloom, 1976; Kumar, 1991) that have synthesized the research on practice, noting a 21 to 44 percent gain in student learning. Specifically, students who practice score between 21 and 44 percent higher on standardized tests than students who do not practice. This result makes sense, of course, because long-term memories are networks of neurons that have been strengthened through repetition. We need our students to practice past perfection to ensure that the memory connections are permanent (Schenck, 2000).

Mental Note: Some information must be overlearned to become permanent.

What Should Be Rehearsed?

Any knowledge—factual, conceptual, or procedural—that is leading students to their target should be rehearsed. The goal, standard, benchmark, or performance descriptor that you are aiming at requires your students to have some long-term retention of the understanding.

Information necessary for both classroom assessments and standardized tests needs to be rehearsed. Some factual and procedural knowledge may be practiced through rote rehearsal. You learned to ride a bike by trying to ride a bike—that is, practicing the skill repeatedly until you perfected it. Factual knowledge such as multiplication tables, states and capitals, and linking verbs may also be practiced through rote rehearsal.

How Should Rehearsal Be Done?

Rehearsal consists of homework, practice, events, and experiences that will store information in multiple memory pathways. Rehearsal must occur at intervals for the best effect, and sleep can be a major factor in how well information will be retained (Stickgold, Whidbee, Schirmer, Patel, & Hobson, 2000).

The rehearsal process may use many of the recoding strategies. For example, identifying similarities and differences, a strategy introduced in Chapter 3, raises student achievement by as much as 45 percent (Marzano, Pickering, & Pollack, 2001). A student who explores similarities and differences has had the opportunity to generate her own understanding.

Let's look at the possibilities of providing students with multiple "episodes" in which a strategy itself is rehearsed. My target is to get my students to be able to identify similarities and differences under many circumstances. If I have a self-contained classroom, I may be able to use the strategy across disciplines.

- I begin in literature class with a short story in which two friends are vying for the same trophy. I ask my students to create a Venn diagram to show the similarities and differences.

- In social science, we compare the responsibilities of community workers.

- In math, we solve a problem in multiple ways and compare the strategies.

- Two songs have similar messages or melodies, and during music instruction, we discuss them.

- Art class offers the opportunity to compare artistic styles or media.

- Another story is read that provides the opportunity to compare the city to the countryside.

- Students draw images of experiences or objects that have both similarities and differences.

- Skits are written and performed characterizing the differences as well as the similarities of two athletes.

- Students write about two important people in their lives, describing how they are similar and what they do for the student that is different from each other.

When Is Enough, Enough?

The nine examples above address several areas, including learning styles, emotions, personal connections, and social interaction. Will these activities succeed at putting this strategy into long-term memory? Each activity should be preceded by reflection time and followed by reflection and reinforcement after it is completed. With such an approach, the concept in this example has then been rehearsed literally or reflectively 27 times. The experiences would be spread over a period of weeks, with some being completed in class and others assigned as homework. In between the episodes, the students would have time to "sleep on it," which should help the storage process (Mateika, Millrood, & Mitru, 2002). If we could peer into the students' brains, we would see networks being set up. (see Figure 5.1).

| **Mental Note: Multiple experiences lead to stronger memories.** | |

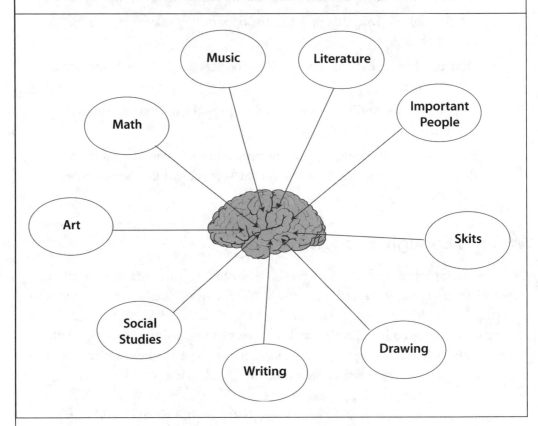

Figure 5.1
Mental Network of the Concept of Similarities and Differences Created Across Disciplines

Rehearsal and Sleep

Teachers are usually eager to find out about the amount of sleep that their students should be having. Almost all raise their hands when I ask if they believe they have students who are sleep deprived. What does sleep have to do with learning?

Many memory researchers agree that memories are encoded during sleep (Schacter, 1996; Stickgold et al., 2000; Mateika, Millrood, & Mitru, 2002).

Stickgold and his colleagues (2000) found that students who slept only six hours after a learning session remembered much less then those who slept a full eight hours. It is suggested that new learning is practiced during sleep. Those networks of neurons that have been formed during learning reconnect during the sleeping process (Blakeslee, 2000).

We all have crammed for an exam at one time or another. We stayed up late going over our notes, awakened early and went over them again, and looked them over right before the test. Many of us were able to store enough information in working memory to do quite well on the test. But we all know that as soon as the test was over, the information was gone. Of course we hadn't stored the information in long-term memory—there wasn't enough sleep to allow the preparation necessary for the neural connections to strengthen to that extent. Research suggests that cutting back on sleep reduces the brain's ability to commit new learning to memory (Dye, 2000).

Mental Note: Cramming is a way to forget rather than remember.

Homework and Practice

The media have suggested that homework is increasing and that students are being robbed of their childhood because of the time spent on it. However, according to Tom Loveless (2003), the director of the Brown Center on Education Policy at the Brookings Institution, "That is not the case." He states that the press was relying on a study completed in 2000 by researchers at the University of Michigan's Population Studies Center. Their results were gleaned from diaries that showed an increase in homework of 23 minutes per week. Loveless believes this increase was due to younger students who never had homework suddenly being assigned homework.

Harris Cooper, a nationally known researcher on homework from Duke University, agrees with Loveless. Cooper says that homework should increase by 10 minutes for every year the student is in school (Viadero, 2003).

The question remains, How important is homework? Marzano, Pickering, and Pollack's (2001) meta-analysis answers this question: The results of homework produce a percentile gain of up to 24 points. So, students who do homework have an advantage on standardized tests over those who do not. Moreover, homework that is graded has higher results: Homework with teacher's comments show a percentile gain of 30, graded homework shows a gain of 28, and homework that is assigned but not commented on or graded shows a gain of only 11.

The National Assessment of Educational Progress published results from a study of its 1994 test ("Good Study Habits," 1997). Three groups of students—4th graders, 8th graders, and 12th graders—were asked the following questions: How much time do you spend on homework? How frequently do you discuss your studies at home? How many pages do you read each day at school and for homework? From the answers and the test scores, the results suggest a positive relationship between good study habits and high test scores.

Several very important points are made regarding homework in *Classroom Instruction That Works* (Marzano, Pickering, & Pollack, 2001) and *The First Days of School* (Wong & Wong, 1991):

- **Homework should be constructed around content with which the students are familiar.** In the chapter on recoding, I state that this process should not be graded and should be done in class, as recoding for homework may be stressful. Students do not know what they know until the recoding and reinforcement steps have taken place. Students need a coach for recoding, but once the content is understood, homework is a valuable tool for rehearsal of that understanding.

- **Homework can be assigned for elaboration of what the students have learned.** Under these circumstances, students have a basic understanding of the material, and the homework offers a new way of using it. For instance, the students understand the concept of cell division, and the teacher assigns homework in which the students find an Internet site describing or demonstrating mitosis.

- **Have specific guidelines for homework.** These guidelines should include some homework tips for students and parents concerning organizing the homework process. Parents should encourage students but limit the amount of help they provide. Homework time should equal 10 times the grade level.

- **Clearly determine and share the purpose of the homework.** Students need to know what the target is that they are aiming for. In mathematics, for instance, the student needs to know whether the homework problems should show all work or whether the answer alone is sufficient. Is the teacher looking for process or product? If prerequisite knowledge will enable the student to do the homework, the teacher should share what the student will need to know to complete the assignment.

- **Reinforce the homework with various types of feedback.** As stated in the reinforcement step, feedback can come from different individuals and in different modes. Students can assess their own work and that of other students, or the teacher can provide the majority of the feedback.

In *Qualities of Effective Teachers*, Strong (2002) states that the quantity of homework is not the key. It is the quality. Strong also reports that homework is more effective in influencing student achievement when it is graded and discussed in class.

> **Mental Note: Homework provides multiple rehearsals and raises student achievement.**

Higher-Level Thinking and Rehearsal

The Cognitive Process Dimension of the revised version of Bloom's taxonomy (Anderson et al., 2001) describes the higher-level thinking skills as analyzing, evaluating, and creating. These are the levels we strive for in teaching. They can be addressed at the rehearsal step in the memory process as well as during the review and retrieve steps.

When we rehearse, we begin by aiming for the cognitive processes of remembering, understanding, and applying. Remembering encompasses recognition and recall. These are lower levels of thinking but nonetheless important. To analyze, evaluate, or create, students must have some information to work with. Therefore, it may be important to begin the rehearsal process with simple recall and recognition tasks for the students. As these neural connections strengthen, students will be able to move to the next level and apply the new information. Anderson and his colleagues (2001) categorize this step as executing and implementing. If procedural knowledge is being learned, this is a crucial step in acquiring a complete understanding and being able to transfer the information. Rehearsal of procedural knowledge may include the application of the procedure to a task with which the student is familiar.

Mr. Bellows has been working with his students on the scientific method. To reach the students, he had several large bowls of popcorn on his desk when the students entered. It had been recently popped, so the aroma in the room was strong. When they asked if they could have some, he explained that before they could enjoy the popcorn, they had to use the scientific method to determine which popcorn popped better and was fluffier and tastier. He further explained that he had popcorn that was homegrown, popcorn from a movie theater, and popcorn from a grocery store. The students came to order quickly, knowing the sooner they figured out the problem, the sooner they could eat!

For reflection, Mr. Bellows asked the students to write in their journals about a popcorn experience that they had. He shared his own experience of burning his hand badly with oil as he poured some popcorn out of a pot. Many of them had never heard of popping popcorn the old-fashioned way. After writing their reflections, the steps to the scientific method were presented on the overhead. The students then had to find a partner and explain those steps before recoding the steps in their own terms. Mr. Bellows cruised the classroom as the students recoded, offering reinforcement and suggestions.

The students formalized the question and created their hypotheses. A hypothesis is a statement using the original research question, so many students used, "I believe that movie theater popcorn will pop better, taste better, and be fluffier." They then listed their materials: the types of popcorn, the popper, oil, and so forth. The procedure was written in a step-by-step manner noting the amount of time it took to pop each type, the fluffiness of the kernels, and, of course, the taste test. Then the students recorded their results and observations. Mr. Bellows requested a reflection section as well.

Once Mr. Bellows was certain that the students understood the scientific method and had a written recoding of the steps as well as the popcorn example, he assigned homework. The assignment was to determine which television channel showed the most commercials.

Through this rehearsal and many others, Mr. Bellows is attempting to elaborate on the procedure and repeat it using relevant and meaningful assignments. When his students encounter an unfamiliar problem, as on the state assessment, they are much more likely to employ the procedure after having had numerous rehearsals.

Analyzing

This step in the taxonomy includes differentiating, organizing, and attributing. *Differentiating* involves separating information into relevant and irrelevant parts and then using only the important parts. Using the scientific method from the previous scenario, students would be analyzing when they read some text and then apply the method to the relevant portions of that text. *Organizing* includes identifying the component parts of a situation or a problem, and then identifying the relationships among relevant elements. Students would take research reports and analyze them in relation to the steps in the scientific method: hypothesis, method, results, and conclusion. *Attributing* involves deconstructing information and checking for values or bias. In the scientific method, students would be able to look at the components and analyze the values or find biases of the authors in the method. These are all possible homework and practice rehearsals for the students.

Evaluating

Using this higher-level thinking skill involves checking and critiquing. Mr. Bellows could have his students examine research reports that used the scientific method and check for inconsistencies. Perhaps the conclusion is not supported by the data, ·or the hypothesis is not a clear result of the research question. The students could then continue by critiquing the reports, noting whether the hypotheses are reasonable or recognizing the positive and negative features of the sample.

Creating

Taking students to this level of thinking involves moving from the ordinary to the original. Considered the highest level of thinking, creating allows the student to plan and produce steps and methods to use in unanticipated situations. Students may generate their own problems to be solved using the scientific method. They may plan a lesson to teach the scientific method. Constructing their own steps to solving problems that do not meet the standard criteria for the scientific method is also a possibility.

Mental Note: For transfer of learning to occur, students must be able to take their knowledge and understandings and use them when confronted with situations and problems that are unexpected or unusual.

Rehearsal and Multiple Memory Pathways: Many Trips Down Memory's Lanes

A working knowledge of the memory pathways—or "lanes," as I called them in my book *Learning and Memory: The Brain in Action* (Sprenger, 1999)—will help identify different rehearsal strategies (see Figure 5.2).

Semantic instruction is what we do most in school. That is, we are trying to take semantic information and help students make permanent connections to it. However, the semantic memory pathway is only one of the many pathways to learning that we have in our brains. The *episodic* pathway stores event and location memories. The *emotional* pathway, the strongest pathway we have, stores our memories for emotional events. According to Cahill (2004), the amygdala, the primitive emotional structure in the limbic area of the brain, most affects what we remember. Its many connections throughout the brain allow it to communicate immediately

Figure 5.2
The Five Memory Lanes

Memory Lane	Strategies
Semantic	Graphic organizers Mind maps Time lines Peer teaching Practice tests
Episodic	Field trips Bulletin boards and posters Decorations Seating arrangements
Emotional	Music Personalization Storytelling Role-play Debate
Procedural	Dance Role-play Body peg systems Cheers Movement while learning (walking, marching)
Conditioned Response (Automatic)	Songs Poems Flash cards Quiz shows

whenever something is important emotionally to remember. The *procedural* pathway is used for muscle memories and basic procedures that we practice repeatedly until they become second nature. Finally, we can condition certain memories by the conditioned-response or *automatic* pathway. Through the rehearsal process, we can take information and store it in many or all of these pathways.

The memory lanes provide multiple possibilities for creating varied experiences for your students. To make the learning transferable, use as many pathways as possible. Keep in mind that your students may need to convey the content through paper-and-pencil tests, such as state standardized tests. If this is the case, be sure to transfer the information to the semantic pathway in writing. With various contexts, students are more likely to abstract the related features of concepts and create a more flexible representation of knowledge (Bransford, Brown, & Cocking, 1999).

In *A Taxonomy for Learning, Teaching, and Assessing* (Anderson et al., 2001), recall and recognition are lower-level skills. We must remember that memory is a somewhat developmental process. According to DeFina (2003), younger children have difficulty conceptualizing complicated curricula. At the age of 7 or 8, students have the ability to retrieve only one item when using a memory cue, but by 10 or 11, that same cue may help retrieve three different items. Recall improves as the students get older. For instance, 80 percent of 5th graders can use categories to organize information and help with retrieval. Then as students progress through school, they develop the ability to organize information using conceptual categories.

This information tells us that the types of rehearsal we use with students will vary according to grade level and ability. Differentiating rehearsal strategies may be one way of meeting the needs of all of our students (Sprenger, 2003). Payne (2001) tells us that all humans think in stories until the age of 7, and thereafter, the brain still prefers to think that way. Our episodes and events comprise our stories. By creating lessons that are unique events in the lives of our students, we can assist with their long-term retention. Making rehearsal an event-filled process will secure knowledge in the episodic pathway and eventually in the semantic pathway (Eichenbaum, 2003). Events usually elicit emotions, and adding emotion to our teaching will also help store information in long-term memory. Rehearsal strategies that engage emotion might include debates, role plays, persuasive writing, interviewing, and campaigning.

What About Mnemonics?

Familiar mnemonic techniques for enhancing memory include peg systems, acronyms, acrostics, the method of loci, chaining, and music and rhythm (see Figure 5.3). Many of these help create visual pictures in our minds.

Mnemonics are based on linking what needs to be learned with what is already known, placing information in multiple pathways, adding attention and interest to what is being taught, and storing with cues to make it easier to find the information. The less prior knowledge you have, the more mnemonics can be helpful. They take an unusual association and make it memorable. Although connections are made in the brain this way, because they are not meaningful, they don't add to the value of the information (Gordon & Berger, 2003).

Using mnemonics for factual information that will need to be recalled is useful. For conceptual understanding, however, more meaningful elaborative rehearsal is suggested. If you expect your students to use memory strategies, you must teach them how to use them. Many strategies are second nature to us now that we are adults, but we were not born with them—they were taught to us. As in any other type of memory, we need to rehearse the rehearsal strategies to get them into long-term memory and have them at our disposal when we need them.

> **Mental Note: Mnemonics are made as a memory aid.**

Mental and Physical Rehearsal

Two more ways to rehearse are possible. The first is mental practice. We have read studies of how athletes and musicians mentally rehearse their play or selection. In the same way, we can practice any type of information. A single mental run-through can be valuable; several are even better. Moreover, it may be more effective to take advantage of auditory memory at the same time and say the information to be remembered aloud (Gordon & Berger, 2003).

Another format for rehearsal is hands-on learning or learning through movement—physical rehearsal. Movement is known to enhance learning by

Figure 5.3
Mnemonic Devices to Aid Memory

Mnemonic	Example/Explanation
Rhyming Peg System	Remembering ordered or unordered items by first memorizing a list of keywords that rhyme with a sequence of digits: • One is sun. • Six is bricks. • Two is shoe. • Seven is heaven. • Three is tree. • Eight is gate. • Four is door. • Nine is line. • Five is hive. • Ten is hen.
Acronyms	A word or phrase made entirely of letters that are cues to words we must remember (e.g., *HOMES* for the Great Lakes: Huron, Ontario, Michigan, Erie, and Superior)
Acrostics	A sentence in which the first letter of each word is a cue. For example, "A Rat In The House Might Eat The Ice Cream"; the first letters spell *arithmetic*.
Method of Loci	Using a place and the objects in it to associate with a list of items. Choose a starting place, and as you go around the room, place the item with the object (e.g., bedroom: dresser is for first item, bed for second, lamp for third, picture for fourth, window for fifth, etc.).
Chaining	Constructing a story that contains each element of a list. For example: items to be remembered are counties in the south of England: Avon, Dorset, Somerset, Cornwall, Wiltshire, Devon, Gloucestershire, Hampshire, and Surrey. An <u>Avon</u> lady came to my <u>Dor</u> and <u>set</u> down her wares. She said she had <u>Some</u> more to <u>set</u>, but the <u>Corn</u> was growing over the <u>wall</u> of her shop. She said that it was making her flowers <u>Wilt</u> and she was <u>shire</u> (sure) that the <u>Dev</u>il was <u>on</u> her trail. She had <u>Glossy</u> teeth with bits of <u>Ham</u> stuck in them. <u>Sure</u> enough, I slammed the door!
Music and Rhythm	Create a song or rhyme for the information to be remembered. A great example: In the movie *Born Yesterday*, the amendments to the Constitution are sung.

adding another dimension and another pathway for storage. Wenglinsky (2002) found that for science, hands-on learning provided the best results. Similarly, math manipulatives have become commonplace for a good reason. They work in helping students learn and remember concepts. Hands-on learning is vital to the child who has the kinesthetic learning style (Sprenger, 2003). Homework and practice should include opportunities to use both body and mind.

3rd Grade Fraction Unit

Standard: Students should develop understanding of fractions as parts of unit wholes, as parts of a collection, and as divisions of whole numbers.

Reach: As math time began, Mr. Rogers asked for a volunteer. Germil raised his hand and was chosen. Mr. Rogers took out a long piece of red yarn. He asked the students, "If I wanted to tie this yarn around Germil to divide him into two halves, where would I tie the yarn?" The students suggested at his waist. He tied the yarn around his waist. "Now what if I wanted to show you one-fourth of him?" The students chose a spot around his shoulders. Mr. Rogers then took out a piece of yarn for each student, and they spent several minutes putting the yarn in various spots to indicate fractions of the person.

Reflect: A PMI chart was chosen. Mr. Rogers had the students draw the chart and fill it in. They were to write what they thought the pluses were about using fractions, then the minuses, and finally what was interesting about fractions. The students took some time doing this as they made connections with prior knowledge.

Recode: For this step, Mr. Rogers had the students write a list of examples in their lives when fractions were helpful. Most students came up with experiences such as sharing a candy bar with a friend, baking a cake, and dividing money from a lemonade stand.

Reinforce: Mr. Rogers cruised the room checking the examples. He cleared up a few misconceptions and gave positive reinforcement to his students.

Rehearsal: Mr. Rogers knew that many rehearsals would be necessary, and he wanted to be sure to move the students to some higher-level thinking. (The rehearsals and the positive attributes of each are presented in Figure 5.4.) He included a reflection or reinforcement step after each rehearsal, too. The students seemed to understand well.

Figure 5.4
Rehearsals for Understanding Fractions

Rehearsal	Memory Enhancers
1. Mr. Rogers brought in small containers of Play-Doh. Students picked three different colors. Then he asked them to pick the first color and remove one-fourth, pick the second color and remove one-third, and take one-half from the final color.	Movement, manipulatives
2. For the second rehearsal, the class used the Play-Doh activity again; however, after removing the fractional amounts, the students discussed the fraction that was left inside the container.	Movement, manipulatives, reasoning
3. The third rehearsal was making a poster of the students' favorite fraction. They wrote their fraction and then drew examples of items that could be cut to get that fraction (e.g., pies, apples, oranges, candy bars, etc.).	Movement, drawing, exemplifying
4. Mr. Rogers brought in the "pies" from the game Trivial Pursuit. He had enough for each student. The pies contained six equal triangles. The students discovered that six-sixths was a whole pie. Then they removed one-third of the pie and talked about the fact that they removed two one-sixth portions and so forth.	Movement, manipulatives, understanding
5. The students walked through the building in pairs to find items that are fractions. For instance, some found a glass of water that was half full, pencils that had been sharpened down to a third of their usual size, and trash cans that were two-thirds full.	Movement, collaboration, real world, understanding
6. Mr. Rogers brought in two whole pizzas. There were 22 students in the class, and, with their teacher, they needed to cut the pizzas to make 23 slices. The students figured out that the fairest way to slice the pizzas was into 12 equal slices for each pizza. The extra slice was given to the principal.	Hands-on, multisensory, real world, understanding
7. As the students were able to apply their knowledge, Mr. Rogers wanted to see if they could work backward by analyzing how much sand was in a bowl. Using the larger spoon first, each pair was to determine how many teaspoons and fractions of teaspoons were in the bowl.	Hands-on, collaboration, analysis, evaluation

Figure 5.4
Rehearsals for Understanding Fractions (continued)

Rehearsal	Memory Enhancers
8. Mr. Rogers brought in a bag of candy for each group of four students. They were to separate the candy by colors. They counted the total number of candies and figured what fraction of the total each color represented. These were snack-size bags, so the number in each was limited.	Collaboration, hands-on, evaluation, analysis, application
9. The students used round circles of colored construction paper. They were to divide the first in half, the second in thirds, the third in fourths, and so forth.	Manipulatives, evaluation, analysis, application
10. The students were given a diagram of a huge ice cream sundae, with 60 scoops in the bowl. Mr. Rogers asked, "If they color 30 scoops chocolate, 20 scoops strawberry, and 10 scoops vanilla, what is the fraction of the whole sundae that each flavor represents?"	Hands-on, deduction, analysis, synthesis, application
11. The students were asked to create their own ice cream sundae and choose the flavors for each scoop. Then they determined the fractional part of the whole sundae each flavor represented.	Creativity, evaluation, analysis, application

From Working Memory to Long-term Retention

Expanding connections for conceptual, procedural, and factual knowledge is the job of rehearsal. By spacing out opportunities to rehearse using multiple memory pathways, students have the opportunity to sleep and enhance the memory storage process. The first four steps in teaching for memory provide the brain with the working memory knowledge and understanding. This fifth step, rehearsal, allows permanent changes to take place in the brain. Solid neural connections can be made in such a way that the possibility of transfer is increased. If information can be stored in all of the memory pathways, then they can be accessed easily through various memory cues.

Reflection

1. Rehearsal is the ideal time to reach all students through their individual learning styles. Homework and practice can be offered in different modalities.

2. Learning in small increments with practice in between is a more accurate way of storing information.

3. Consider each practice or rehearsal an episode. Take into account the environment in which you are teaching. Making your instruction more unique through posters, pictures, and varied room arrangements may help with storage and retrieval of information.

4. Encourage students to implement their own rehearsals. Rehearsing new material each night before bedtime for just a few minutes can increase retention.

Review

Without review, most information will be lost from memory.

Cramming seeks to stamp things in by intense application immediately before the ordeal. But a thing thus learned can form but few associations.

—William James, Talks to Teachers

It's the day before the test on insects. My friend and colleague, Laurel, looks at her lesson plan book. Across the top of the page in bold letters is the word REVIEW. She thinks, "I have been so busy with all of these insect activities that I haven't even looked at the assessment. Our school has a brand-new textbook series, and the publisher has provided assessments."

Laurel walks over to the filing cabinet and pulls out the "Insect" folder. She finds several worksheets that she didn't bother using. She's been teaching this unit for years and has enough material to keep her students busy learning all day long. She grabs the sheet that says "Postassessment." She is startled by that title. That means there must have been a pre-assessment, and she doesn't think she used that. "Oh, well," she tells herself, "I'll just look this over and make sure I covered everything." Much to her dismay, the publisher's test not only covered material that she hadn't but also left out some information that she thought was important. She digs deeper into her cabinet to find the assessment she gave her 3rd graders last year. In comparing the two, she decides the publisher's test better addresses the material that was taught. Now, what? She looks at her schedule and thinks about her plans from after school until bedtime. Does she have the time and energy to create a new assessment? Should she delay the test? The answer to each is no. The day after tomorrow she is attending a workshop, and she doesn't want to have a substitute give the test. She decides to teach the material on the test that she didn't cover during her review. After all, this information was in the text that the students were supposed to read.

You can guess the results. This is something we probably all have done at some time in our careers—before we understood the brain and how kids learn and remember. This was review: a session a day or two before the test in which either the teacher went over what was on the assessment, or the teacher asked the students if they had any questions on the material. Especially at the middle and high school levels, I was always amazed at the short review sessions I had—and then I was disappointed at the test scores. It didn't take me too long until I learned an important fact: Kids don't know what they don't know. So, asking them for their questions was a total waste of time. The only students who would come up with a question were the ones who knew the material well enough to ask about a particular nuance.

 Mental Note: Kids don't know what they don't know.

Why Review?

Review is actually a reconsideration of the learning. With the multiple experiences we give our students in the rehearsal stage, there may be little need for review if the assessment follows those rehearsals. We do want our students to remember material later, perhaps for a comprehensive examination or a standardized test. In these cases, review becomes even more important.

Schacter's (2001) discussion about the "sins" of memory underscores the importance of review. Among the seven sins he discusses, three to be aware of in the classroom are blocking, misattribution, and transience.

Blocking occurs when the information is stored but cannot be accessed. We've all had the experience of seeing a former student and being unable to recall her name. This is sometimes called the "tip of the tongue" phenomenon. We know the name and just can't quite spit it out. Yet a short while later, the name comes easily to us. This occurs with our students as well. They know the answer, but in an assessment situation, they can't access it. Blocking often arises with proper nouns: names of people, places, documents, and other material with a specific name. Interestingly, common nouns usually have synonyms that we can substitute for the word (Schacter, 2001). If a student is writing an essay about the war in Vietnam, for example, and wants to tell about *combat* but can't recall that word, he can use *battle* or *struggle* instead. The name of the battle, however, is not replaceable. Frequent review may help alleviate the probability of blocking.

Misattribution is attributing a memory to the wrong situation or source; thus it is also sometimes described as *source memory problems*. Misattribution is particularly common in students. Until the frontal lobes are fully developed, they often have difficulty in discerning their sources of information (Zola, 2002).

I am teaching my students about the brain. We are discussing the hypothalamus, the structure below the thalamus that contains nerve connections that send messages to the pituitary gland and therefore plays a role in body temperature, emotions, hunger, thirst, circadian rhythms, and hormones. It is also responsible for fat metabolism. On the bus after school, some of my students are discussing their brains. The girls agree that the hypothalamus regulates their hunger and talk about diet drugs and exercise to control weight. One of the boys sitting close by mentions that he read in a fitness magazine that the hippocampus responds by producing new neurons whenever you exercise.

A few days later, I give my students a practice test on the brain material. This test is not for a grade; it is more of a recoding strategy to allow more reinforcement and correction. It also gives them the opportunity to transfer information that may be stored in other pathways to the semantic pathway. Part of the assessment is multiple-choice, and one of the questions is "The structure most likely to affect and be affected by diet and exercise is (a) the amygdala, (b) the thalamus, (c) the hippocampus, or (d) the hypothalamus." Most of the students answer that question quickly by marking (d), hypothalamus, but two of the girls and one boy involved in that bus conversation answered (c), hippocampus. Why?

They remembered bits of the conversation about the hippocampus and exercise and con-fused the source—they thought I had given them that information.

Had I given them a review before the practice test, this problem may not have occurred. We would have reexamined the structures and functions and possibly erased the misconception from their brains. Because the test was only for practice, the analysis of the test answers served as a review and corrected their misplaced source information.

Transience, sometimes referred to as the *forgetting curve* or the *fading theory*, refers to a memory being lost over time. This theory suggests that the neural con-nections in the brain will weaken without use; in other words, "Use it or lose it!" Several studies have been done examining how quickly information fades from memory. The results from one such study with textbook material (Keeley, 1997) are interesting:

- 54 percent of the material was remembered after 1 day;

- 35 percent of the material was remembered after 7 days;

- 21 percent of the material was remembered after 14 days;

- 8 percent of the material was remembered after 21 days.

Another study done on the memory of a lecture found that after 14 days, partici-pants forgot 90 percent of the information (Keeley, 1997)!

These studies all support the importance of multiple rehearsals over time and spaced reviews. According to Schenck (2000), spacing reviews throughout the learning and increasing the time between them gradually allows long-term net-works to be strengthened. For both traditional testing and standardized testing, the timing between repeated reviews can significantly affect how much information is retained. In Schenck's research, he found that typical test review takes place long after the initial learning and rehearsal. He suggests that we review from the begin-ning with short intervals in between. Then we should increase the time between reviews (see Figure 6.1).

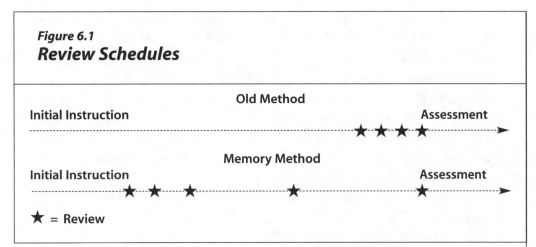

Figure 6.1
Review Schedules

Adapted from Schenck (2000).

Mental Note: Without review, important information may be lost.

Jane, our science teacher, is covering a unit on volcanoes. Her target is an objective for earth science: Knows how land forms are created through a combination of constructive and destructive forces. Constructive forces include crustal deformation, volcanoes, and deposition of sediment; destructive forces include weathering and erosion. The students have created visuals of the vocabulary words, discussed and written about "the year without a summer, 1816," seen video clips of volcanoes, have done a PMI chart, and looked at and discussed pictures of Jane's trip to Hawaii and her visit to a volcano. All of this took, with interruptions of school assemblies, one week. Her next "experience" for the students is to take a field trip to the science museum to learn about predicting volcanoes.

Before the trip, Jane will conduct her first review. She wants to be sure that the students have a conceptual understanding. She has written a selected response test for this unit, so she wants her reviews to match the assessment. To reach her students, Jane chooses a Trivial Pursuit game for review. She hasn't come up with the questions for it; she's going to divide the students into two groups and have them create the questions for the other team. Some of the questions the students design are multiple-choice, and others are short-answer. She is delighted because these formats will closely match her assessment. The students enjoy both aspects of this review, creating and participating. Jane gives them feedback on the questions they miss that they do not understand. They are ready for the field trip!

The day of the trip, Jane hands out a graphic organizer for the students to jot down the steps they will be learning. The day after the field trip, when she sees the students again, they will do a four-corner reflection of the trip and share their organizers in small groups. The following day, Jane has the students do research in pairs. Using the Internet, the students will research a famous volcanic eruption in history, determine the scientific evidence that was available at the time for predictions, and write about the impact the eruption had on the civilization surrounding it. This project takes several days.

Knowing that memory is fragile, Jane plans another review. This time she chooses a mind map that the class can create together using colored markers and butcher paper on the bulletin board. They begin with the word Volcanoes in the middle of the paper and enclose it in a cloud—"a cloud of volcanic dust," as they called it. Jane calls on only those who wish to participate, and the students, taking turns, draw major detail lines and write briefly what that detail is. They then create a symbol or picture for it. Subtopics, details, and vocabulary words are written in the same color marker below the line. Jane prompts them using multiple-choice questions to remain aligned with her assessment. They complete the mind map that Jane can now use and add to for her next review.

The unit continues with problem solving. Jane addresses the temperature of lava and asks students to figure out the following: Lava pouring out of the lava tube is about 1,150 degrees Celsius. How hot is the lava in Fahrenheit?

The unit ends a few weeks later. Jane has had three reviews of the material before the final assessment. Her students do very well.

According to Schenck (2000), if students have been actively involved in their learning and review takes place two or three weeks later, the students should retain most of the knowledge for two to three months.

Mental Note: Review can increase the length of time that students remember.

Reprinted with permission from Marshall Ramsey and Copley News Service.

How Do We Review?

Review of factual information may be a matter of reorganization. Remember that we are taking information from long-term memory, bringing it into working memory, examining it to ensure accuracy, and taking an opportunity perhaps to reorganize it to enhance transfer. I have the following goals with any review:

- Match the review to instruction and assessment.
- Check for accuracy of the memory.
- Give students the conditions to use higher-level thinking skills to analyze, evaluate, and possibly create alternative ways to use the knowledge.
- Strengthen the existing networks.
- For high-stakes testing, practice similar questions under similar conditions.
- Eliminate cramming.

The three strategies that ACT (2004) recommends for its test preparation are (1) familiarize yourself with the content of the ACT tests, (2) refresh your knowledge and skills in the content areas, and (3) identify the content areas you have not studied.

If review is done intermittently, as previously suggested, then we may be able to avoid students cramming right before the test. In a research study at the University of Ohio, Tuckman (1998) found that learners who procrastinate performed better on final exams when frequent quizzes had been given. These results are similar to those of a study by Wenglinsky (2002), who found that students whose teachers periodically gave them paper-and-pencil tests scored higher on standardized tests.

Several researchers suggest that cramming close to test time may indeed raise test scores (Vacha & McBride, 1993; Crew, 1969; Schenck, 2000). For example, Crew (1969) found that students who crammed for the test the day before for two hours scored considerably higher than the students who did not. After the test, however, students who crammed did not retain the knowledge.

Pop Quizzes

Having created brain-compatible classrooms for 15 years, I had dismissed the notion of the pop quiz. After all, an unannounced quiz can cause stress, and I wanted my classroom to be as stress-free as possible.

Last summer, though, I changed my mind. I was conducting a five-day workshop based on my book *Becoming a Wiz at Brain-Based Teaching* (Sprenger, 2002). There were 70 participants including K–12 teachers, specialists, school psychologists, and administrators. When the discussion of stress began, I shared ways of de-stressing the classroom such as incorporating music and plenty of ritual, teaching like a coach, and using clear targets and rubrics. When asked how I felt about pop quizzes, I replied that I no longer used them because I felt they raised students' stress levels too much. At the break, a high school Spanish teacher approached me looking quite concerned. He said he gave pop quizzes regularly. He liked them because the kids did their assignments and practiced to keep up their grades. He was wondering if he should change his whole approach. We decided we would both do some research before the end of the week and discuss it.

I was surprised at the research I found. Graham (1999), for example, studied four psychology classes that were given pop quizzes over the course of two semesters. Tests given after the quizzes were half a grade higher than scores from classes that did not get quizzes. The students were actually motivated by the quizzes. I believe that in both situations, this study and the Spanish teacher's class, the pop quizzes were often enough to become part of the class ritual. Therefore, expecting those quizzes and preparing for them may have relieved some of the stress.

> **Mental Note: Quizzes as review may increase test scores on subsequent examinations.**

Other Ways to Review

Factual information may be reviewed differently than conceptual information. For things such as formulas, definitions, or lists of information, students may want to make flash cards for review, put the information to music or chant, or review with rote repetition. These will access different memory pathways as described in chapter 5.

Conceptual information needs more comprehensive review. Mind mapping, one of the strategies used earlier in the chapter, is one of my favorite review tools (see Figure 6.2 for a mind map on how to create a mind map). I arrange my students in teams for this activity. On the review day, I have a 12- by 18-inch sheet of construction paper for each group. They get out their markers, and I ask them to create a mind map of the concepts that we are covering. If we are using a text, they may use that, their notes, and any of the recoding and rehearsal materials they have. In groups, students usually finish this task in 20 or 30 minutes. Then the maps are put up on a wall or bulletin board for all to see. The students examine each other's maps and may add to their map if they see that it is missing important information. As I said earlier, my students don't know what they don't know. But after this activity, they do. This is when they ask questions, and I provide feedback and reinforcement for them.

Other reviews might include webs, concept maps, note taking, and checklists. Try to create the same environment the students will have for the testing. If the assessment has open-ended questions, so should the review. If recognition memory is going to be employed, make recognizing answers part of the review. Take this opportunity to make some real-world applications with the material. You have probably done this through some of the rehearsal strategies you used, but offering

Figure 6.2
A Mind Map Indicating How to Make a Mind Map

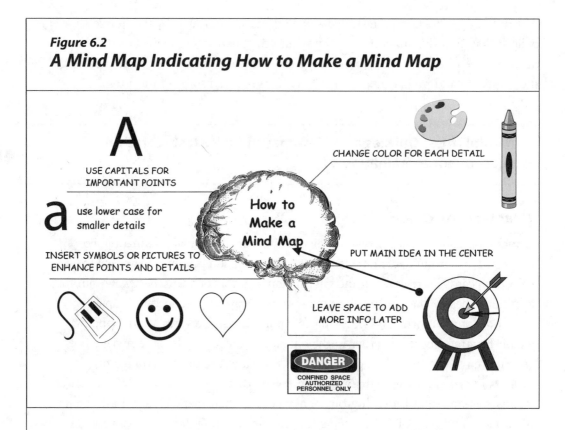

a problem or situation that is relevant to the students and follows the same "game plan" as previous rehearsals will be helpful. Be sure to refer to the rehearsals that you have used. This will spark some memories as well as provide practice.

Procedural review involves more application, evaluation, and analysis. If the students have learned a skill, they should practice the skill in the manner in which they will be tested. If the assessment is paper-and-pencil, you must assist them in making the transfer to the semantic pathway. For instance, if they spent most of their rehearsals using math manipulatives, but you are going to give them a written test with problems to solve, you need to spend time helping them transfer what they learned to paper. You can assist this process by reminding them what they did with the manipulatives. Perhaps they can visualize the process and practice applying it on paper. This is probably one of the gaps we see in achievement, the inability to transfer process and product to paper. If I asked you to tell me how to tie a shoe without using your hands or looking at your feet, you would be able to do it, but with some difficulty or discomfort. You would have to use some brain-power to transfer this information that is conveniently stored in your procedural pathway to the semantic pathway to explain. With practice you could do so quickly and easily, but in the beginning it takes time and effort. So it is with our students who are trying to transfer. Any emotional connections that your students may have to the learning should be included in the review. If you reached your students through the emotional pathway when you introduced the knowledge, remind them of it during the review. Any emotional moments throughout the lessons or unit when there was laughter, excitement, or sadness may trigger memories. Every time we recall something, we are rehearsing or reviewing it. The review step is the chance to let your students "call up" the memories that they will need for the assessment—or for life!

> **Mental Note: Emotions that were engaged during instruction and rehearsal should be engaged during review.**

Review, Transfer, and Higher-Level Thinking

From the rehearsal step, our students should have plenty of conceptual information, as well as simple facts, stored in long-term memory. The review, then, may be a time for climbing the new taxonomy by analyzing, evaluating, and creating. You may ask your students to take their new long-term understandings and separate relevant from irrelevant material. Perhaps they can take themes, morals, or lessons learned and apply them to their own lives. When studying *Julius Caesar,* for instance, students analyze Brutus and Cassius while comparing them to present-day individuals. During a review on consumerism, students create commercials that show their conceptual understanding of media influences. Perhaps, in a social science review, students evaluate individual battles and their contributions to the war effort.

Teaching for Memory: An Example Using *The Giver* by Lois Lowry

Mrs. Fox had followed her plans carefully. Using a backward design model, she began with what she wanted the students to know. She then developed an assessment that would let them show her that they had learned, retained, and could transfer information. She was certain her students had long-term storage for her unit on the novel The Giver *by Lois Lowry. She has more than one recoding session, because she wants her students to consider several themes. Her unit design looked like this:*

Reach #1: When the students enter the classroom, they must choose whether to sit on the side of the room labeled "Here" or on the other side labeled "Elsewhere." They are not allowed to ask questions until all are seated. They brainstorm ideas about the differences between Here and Elsewhere. The students begin reading the book.

Reflection #1: The students will write in the journals about how they feel about the unknown. What if they were leaving to go Elsewhere?

Reach #2: On day 2, the students enter the room, where the song "Memories" is playing. The students are asked to think of their favorite memories and share them with others.

Reflection #2: Students label a page in their journal "Memories." They are to write as many important memories as they can in five minutes. The reading continues.

Recode: The students write examples of the importance of memory and survival in the story. They will compare and contrast a life without memory and without pain to a life with both.

Reinforce: Through Socratic questioning, Mrs. Fox will clear up any misunderstandings the students may have. All ideas will be written on the board and considered.

Rehearsal #1: To get information into the procedural memory pathway, students will role-play several scenes from the novel.

Rehearsal #2: After discussing the definitions of similes and metaphors, students will write three of their own using Gabriel, Jonas, and the concept of release.

Rehearsal #3: *Students will compare and contrast our society to the society in the novel.*

Rehearsal #4: *Students will make posters of their world in black and white. The posters will be hung, and students will talk in groups about the importance or necessity of color.*

Rehearsal #5: *Students will write the story of* The Giver *as a news article. This exercise will ensure that the basic facts of the story are clear in their minds.*

Review: *This is an excellent spot to review. The news articles should receive feedback as to their accuracy. Then editorials will be written with views on the articles. Students will exchange news articles and write an editorial based on a classmate's article. Feedback will be provided on the editorial as well.*

Rehearsal #6: *Having completed a Holocaust unit earlier in the year, the students will compare extinction efforts in history. They will bring in information from the previous unit and make text-to-text and text-to-world connections.*

Rehearsal #7: *To offer analysis, evaluation, and creativity, the students will write either a prequel or a sequel of the story.*

Rehearsal #8: *Certain social issues are worth investigating and using as examples and comparisons in the story. The students will do research on the Internet on one of the following topics: day care, surrogate mothers, euthanasia, or volunteerism.*

These rehearsals take several class periods and require homework in most cases. Mrs. Fox will have students discuss each project in small or large groups. After the eight rehearsals and the review, Mrs. Fox may want to test her students' long-term memory. A paper-and-pencil assessment in the form of a practice quiz might give her some of the information she is seeking. The questions should be recall; here are some examples:

1. In *The Giver,* is everyone equal? Is everyone the same? Explain the difference between equal and same.

2. The concept of release is important in Jonas's community. What are the advantages of this concept? Are there disadvantages? What specific examples can provide proof for your answers?

3. Compare our society to Jonas's. What are the advantages of each?

4. Differences between men and women are different in Jonas's society than in ours. What customs do they have to distinguish differences between the two?

If some students do poorly, Mrs. Fox will then want to check to see whether this performance indicates a storage problem or a retrieval problem. She can then offer a recognition test consisting of matching, true/false, and multiple-choice questions.

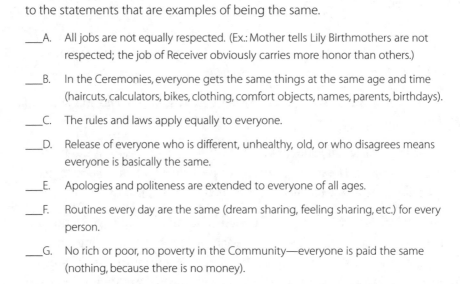

Place an *E* next to the statements that are examples of being equal and an *S* next to the statements that are examples of being the same.

___A.   All jobs are not equally respected. (Ex.: Mother tells Lily Birthmothers are not respected; the job of Receiver obviously carries more honor than others.)

___B.   In the Ceremonies, everyone gets the same things at the same age and time (haircuts, calculators, bikes, clothing, comfort objects, names, parents, birthdays).

___C.   The rules and laws apply equally to everyone.

___D.   Release of everyone who is different, unhealthy, old, or who disagrees means everyone is basically the same.

___E.   Apologies and politeness are extended to everyone of all ages.

___F.   Routines every day are the same (dream sharing, feeling sharing, etc.) for every person.

___G.   No rich or poor, no poverty in the Community—everyone is paid the same (nothing, because there is no money).

With these and other recognition questions, a great deal can be revealed. The students who do not do well on the recall test and perform better on the recognition test are having a retrieval problem. The information is stored because they can recognize it when they see it. For these students, Mrs. Fox will find activities that will help them access the information. Those who do not do well on the recognition test have a storage problem (Mason & Kohn, 2001). This information is not in their long-term memory. This could be due to inattentiveness or lack of sleep, or the students may just need more time and more rehearsals.

> **Mental Note: If students can't recall or recognize, it's a storage problem. If they can recognize but not recall, it's a retrieval problem.**

Reteaching

Review may show us that our students were unable to store information in long-term memory or that it is difficult to retrieve. When reteaching is necessary, the suggestions of a study by Crowley and Siegler (1999) may be helpful. They found that comprehension increases when students first receive a visual demonstration of new learning. Then a verbal explanation follows from someone else. Finally, the recoding strategy is implemented, a reiteration of the material in the learner's own words. Even though you started out in this way when you followed the steps for memory, this shortened version makes more sense at this point in the process. Because some of your students will not need the reteaching component, perhaps they can be the teachers. This exercise will reinforce their learning as it provides new and varied experiences for the learners in need.

Other scientifically researched strategies from the Northwest Regional Education Laboratory (2002) include the following:

- Use engaging materials for remediation, such as "talking software" and age-appropriate reading content.
- Reteach only the priority lesson content until students can show you that they have learned it.
- Address learning style differences more emphatically during reteaching.
- Use different materials and examples for reteaching; this is more than a repeat of previously taught lessons.

> **Mental Note: Reteaching should be a productive experience for all.**

Review of Test-Taking Strategies

I once heard a speaker say that teachers attempt "assumicide." We assume that our students have prior knowledge. We assume that they have memory strategies. We assume that they understand. And we assume that they know how to take a test. Research suggests otherwise.

Casanova and Berliner (1986) recommend that training students in test-taking strategies be done annually. The effects seem to go down shortly after training. They concluded that "for two hours of instruction, a student at the 50th percentile would end up at the 55th." With 3.2 hours of training, the gain in percentile rank goes up to 8; with 5 hours, the gain is 10; and 30 hours equals a gain of 19 percent. Bangert-Drowns, Kulik, and Kulik (1983) suggest that coaching students for test taking raises their scores from the 50th to the 60th percentile. From this research, it appears that we should take some time to review test-taking strategies.

If's for Review

- If the font or print size on the test is going to be different from what your students are accustomed to, use that font and print size for the reviews.

- If the test is going to be timed, review and practice using that time limit.

- If the seating must be in a special pattern, have your students sit in that pattern for several days prior to the test.

- If the students are accustomed to having music in the background when they take classroom assessments, but music is not allowed on the standardized test, give them practice tests without music.

- If some of your students are sound-sensitive, suggest that everyone (even teachers) wear soft-soled shoes or sneakers.

Mental Note: Provide instruction in study skills, such as paraphrasing, outlining, guided note taking, developing cognitive maps, and using advance organizers.

Review: Retrieving, Reworking, and Re-storing Memories

Review encourages our students to retrieve memories from long-term storage areas. It provides more practice in accessing memories and manipulating them in new ways in working memory. Every time we access a memory, we are more likely to be able to access it again. We can continue to call on higher levels of thinking by asking students to recall conceptual understandings and apply them in different situations.

If we are preparing students for standardized testing, we are teaching them the essentials of certain goals, standards, and benchmarks. The test makers will determine in what way our students will show what they know. Because we have little control over that, the more wide-ranging rehearsals and reviews may provide the circumstances under which goals and standards will be assessed. Multiple coding will make access to long-term memories easier (Squire & Kandel, 1999).

Teaching to create accessible memories is a continual process of storage, retrieval, and storing again. As we vary our rehearsals and reviews, we provide new "storerooms" for our memories.

Reflection

1. When you plan your unit, plan your reviews. Space them in the manner suggested in Figure 6.1.

2. Some factual information may require rote memorization. If you have students who have trouble with facts, recommend the mnemonics from chapter 5.

3. With time being our biggest enemy, reviewing often may appear to be time-consuming; however, spaced reviewing may save time in the long run.

4. Review strengthens long-term memory connections. How can you increase the frequency of review in your class?

Retrieve

Memory retrieval may be dependent on cues.

Having a strong memory in storage does not guarantee that you will later
retrieve the memory successfully.

—*Larry Squire and Eric Kandel*, Memory: From Mind to Molecules

*You are driving to work (implicit procedural memory). The bell is ringing as you
arrive, and you jump out of the car and dash into the building (implicit stimulus
response). You enter your classroom, switch on the lights, boot up the computer,
and turn on the music (implicit procedural memory). Two students dash in and
tell you they have to help in the office for a few minutes. Would you please order
hot lunch for them? You repeat their names and their lunch requests over and over
(immediate semantic memory). The other students are seated, and you look over
the class to take attendance. There is an empty seat. You close your eyes to picture
who sits there (explicit episodic memory). Aha! It's Charles. You remember that
Charles told you he had a dental appointment today (explicit, semantic), and it
reminds you of your last trip to the dentist for your root canal. You cringe at the
thought (implicit, emotional). You say it is time for the Pledge of Allegiance, and
your class immediately rises (implicit, procedural). You then recall that last night's*

homework must be turned in and ask your students to pass their papers in (explicit, semantic). They begin to pass their papers up the row to the first person sitting there (implicit, procedural).

As you can see from this scenario, you are constantly retrieving different types of memories. That's how your brain functions on a regular basis. It naturally draws upon what connections it can make for the current situation. According to Pinker (1999), our brains will logically access memories that are useful, that have been repeated, and that require the least effort. Because memory works this way, it is imperative to take our students through the seven steps to provide the necessary repetition and ensure that memories become easy to access. Otherwise, the semantic memories that students require for assessment will be too difficult or impossible to access.

In step 7, retrieval, we will look at several factors affecting how well our students retrieve information. False memory, test anxiety, instruction/assessment mismatch, and location can each influence the ability to retrieve long-term memories.

What Is Retrieval?

Retrieval of memory in its most universal form is the ability to bring a past event or prior knowledge to one's mind. It is this conscious recollection that we call *memory*. Oftentimes this is called *declarative memory* because we can declare it (Squire & Kandel, 1999). Real-life acts of memory usually involve deciding what kind of information is useful at the moment and then selecting that information out of all that we know. We make these decisions all day long (Goldberg, 2001). Again, the scenario that opened this chapter is an example.

When we test our students for facts, *we* are making the decision of what they are to recall. For instance, I may give a basic memory test to participants at a presentation. I may offer them a list of words, ask them to remember them, and then later ask them to write them down. When the decision of what is to be remembered is given to the *participant*, we add higher-level thinking processes. The frontal lobes are involved in the decision.

The 4th grade students have been studying the Civil War. Their teacher, Miss Dees, has been focusing on identifying similarities and differences. She has guided the students through several Venn diagrams using generals, battles, uniforms, forms of fighting, and reasons for fighting as some of the areas investigated. The students write a reflection paper to go with each visual representation.

Miss Dees uses several formative assessments throughout the unit. Students present their diagrams with a brief oral presentation. She gives a vocabulary quiz to ascertain whether they understand the important words in the unit. For her summative assessment at the end of the unit, she wants to assess their understanding. The students have performed well on the individual assessments, and now Miss Dees wants to uncover their ability to take the memories and use them by applying them in a different way.

The assessment begins with this information: "You have been using Venn diagrams to represent the differences and similarities between various aspects of the Civil War. One of the areas we studied was the boredom that soldiers suffered when they were not in battle. Compare and contrast what the soldiers in the Civil War did to handle their boredom with the ways that you use to alleviate boredom."

Miss Dees was the decision maker in the vocabulary quiz. The students knew exactly what they were to study or memorize. For the oral presentation, the students could use higher levels of thinking to create and make their presentations. They chose the similarities and differences. In the last assessment, decision making again went to the students. The assignment does not specifically say to use a Venn diagram; however, many did so. Others created a Venn as a prewriting component and then wrote a paragraph. For this higher-level assessment, the students had to access the procedural knowledge of identifying similarities and differences and their conceptual knowledge of what boredom is and how it is encountered and acted upon in two different aspects of life, in two eras in history, and in some cases by two different age groups.

Mental Note: *Retrieval* **is the ability to access long-term memories, bring then into the working memory process, and solve problems.**

How Do We Retrieve?

Many people claim that they have trouble accessing memories. We know from previous steps that you cannot recall information that you never stored. Active participation encourages learning and memory storage, whereas inattention does not. Where there is no storage, there can be no retrieval. If no effort is being made to record new information for later, then our interests and preferences influence the strength and even the nature of the memory. When we wish to remember, intending to hold onto information for a later result, the probability of having a lasting memory is increased (Squire & Kandel, 1999).

According to Squire and Kandel (1999), "Memory appears to be stored in the same distributed assembly of brain structures that are engaged in initially perceiving and processing what is to be remembered" (p. 72). These neuroscientists suggest that the availability of the memory may depend on the *strength* of the cue provided. If one is asked to recall the plot of a novel recently read by being offered the cue "You know, the one about the woman whose husband dies and she marries that guy?" the cues offered are woman, dead husband, and second marriage. That may seem like enough triggers to jog one's memory, but many novels have similar plots. If the remember is to differentiate one novel from another, dissimilar characteristics are necessary. According to Sousa (2001), "We tend to store information in networks by similarity but retrieve it back into working memory by difference" (p. 142). Therefore, more specific cues may be necessary to remember which novel is being discussed. Perhaps, "Do you remember the novel where the woman lost her husband in the Civil War? She was from the South, and later she marries a Northerner?" These added details offer some of the specific attributes of the novel.

False Memories

It's a simple test. I read a list of words to my students at an average pace. I ask them not to write down any of the words but rather to just sit back and listen. They will not be asked to write down as many as they can remember.

"Blanket, snore, sofa, lullaby, doze, awake, snooze, slumber, peace, yawn, drowsy, dream, tired." I look up from my list and chat with them for about 20 seconds to let the echo of my words pass from their immediate memory.

"OK, raise your hand if you heard me say the word door," I ask. No one raises a hand. "Good. I didn't say the word door. Raise your hand if you heard me say the word awake. A few students raise their hands. I nod, "Yes, I did say the word awake. Raise your hand if you heard me say the word sleep."

With this question, almost every hand is raised. I shake my head. "I didn't say the word sleep." At this the students are amazed.

"What made you believe I said sleep?" I ask.

"You tricked us," Blair says. "You said a lot of words that we think of in relation to sleep."

Blair was correct. What she did not realize was that I intentionally gave my students a false memory. I activated the network of neurons that have been organized in their brains around the concept of sleep. Because I mentioned so many cues for sleep, they believed they had heard it.

This activity was one I had seen Daniel Schacter do many times during his presentations. Giving false memories to others may be difficult to avoid at all times. But it is something we must be aware of when it comes to memory retrieval and assessments. Forced-choice assessments consisting of multiple-choice and true/false questions may easily lead students to a false memory.

Another activity that shows how easily we are swayed by the activated networks in memory storage is as follows: Tell your students that you are going to give them 10 quick questions and they are to answer orally as quickly as possible. Then promptly ask the following two questions: Holding up a sheet white paper, ask, "What color is this paper?" In unison they will all say white. Then quickly ask, "What do cows drink?" Most will answer milk. They then realize their mistake and discussion follows as to why that happens. During a timed test, a network could be activated and cause similar mistakes.

Remind your students to read test questions carefully. If they are multiple-choice, each possible answer must be read in its entirety. These questions begin with a stem and then offer several choices, usually three or four. Only one is the best answer; the others are called *distracters*. And they are meant to do just that—distract the test taker. They may consist of partially correct answers. If the correct part is at the beginning of the distracter, it may activate a network with inaccurate information that causes the student to mark it as the right answer.

Similar situations may occur with true/false questions. It is possible to start each statement with a truth or partial truth, but the ending makes the difference. These types of questions also should be read entirely to ensure accuracy.

Mental Note: Activating networks of neurons may elicit false connections in your students' minds.

Test Anxiety

Test anxiety is a form of stress. Many of us have *eustress*, or good stress, when we take an exam. It gets some adrenaline pumping and actually assists in our recovery of memories. Some students, however, can become overwhelmed by test anxiety.

According to Sapolsky (1998), stress is better handled when five factors are present. The first is predictability. Do students know what kind of assessment they are facing? Are they familiar with the content? Have there been enough rehearsals and reviews? Stiggins (2001) suggests that students be involved in assessments, describing several ways to do so (see Figure 7.1). Choice is another strong component of handling stress. Are there any options for the student? This may be as simple as offering three essay questions but only requiring that two be answered. A feeling of control is the next factor. This can be gained from self-confidence that the student understands the goal of the assessment and has rehearsed and reviewed properly. Social interaction also reduces stress. If the environment is such that the students feel that they are "in this together," they will feel less threatened by a test. Perhaps at times students can take group assessments when appropriate. Finally, physical activity reduces stress. Of course, we don't want students jumping around during a test, but it might be wise to offer some movement activities before testing.

With a student who has fears of test taking, talking with the student and naming those fears may help you provide the student with some strategies for overcoming the specific fear. If the student is afraid of forgetting, perhaps some mnemonics will provide some confidence. If the fear revolves around difficult questions, tell the student to answer the easiest first. Some students are stressed about time limits.

Figure 7.1
Levels of Student Involvement with Assessment

Low-Level Involvement ————————————————→ High-Level Involvement

Takes assess- ment/ gets grade	Is allowed to offer comments on test improve- ment	Proposes possible assess- ment tasks	Constructs assess- ment tasks	Assists with scoring criteria	Creates scoring standard	Self- evaluates using scoring measures	Under- stands assess- ment/ evaluation effects	Relates teacher assessment and self- assessment to academic achievement

Adapted from Stiggins (2001).

Pacing is an important part of testing. Standardized tests are usually timed, and classroom assessments are often given under some time constraints. It is important during reviews to provide students with some possible pacing instructions or give them timed tests (Chapman & King, 2000).

 Mental Note: Discuss with your students ways to deal with test anxiety.

Instruction/Review/Assessment Mismatch

One common problem with retrieval occurs when the instructional strategies used do not match the reviews and/or the assessment. Different vocabulary, levels of complexity, attention spans, or a transfer problem from one memory pathway to another can cause this difficulty.

Vocabulary

The vocabulary issue affects both standardized and classroom assessments. In the former, high-frequency words are used that may be unfamiliar to many of our students. Popham (2001) states in *The Truth About Testing* that children from afflu-ent, educationally oriented families "grow up routinely hearing the words and phrases that form the items on standardized achievement tests. That's especially true if the test deals with language arts, where you'll find item after item in which the child who grew up in a family where 'proper' English was used has a tremen-dous leg up over children whose parents' first language wasn't English or whose parents spoke English in a 'non-standard' manner" (p. 57).

For classroom assessment, we must keep in mind that our verbal vocabulary may or may not be in the memory lexicon of our students. Hearing us use words that they do not see in print until the assessment may confuse and disorient our students. They must also be able to pronounce the words themselves if we want them to use them in a recall exercise or recognize them on a recognition test (Schenck, 2000). For our young or struggling readers, this point is very important.

Susan is working hard in her 6th grade classroom and on her master's program. The course her cohort is taking this semester is on curriculum alignment. For her next class, Susan is to bring in a classroom assessment that can be reviewed by the group. It must match the state standards and meet certain criteria.

Susan is just finishing a novel unit on Wringer *by Jerry Spinelli. She is preparing the final assessment, a paper-and-pencil test. An anticipation guide was used to begin the novel unit. The students have discussed the chapters in small groups, generated their own questions, role-played some of the scenes, and have had large-group discussions. Her class understands the facts, like knowing that a wringer in this story is what a boy turning 10 is called when he is expected to wring the necks of pigeons at the town's annual Pigeon Day. She is certain that the students understand the novel's underlying theme of coming of age. She creates her assessment with some of the following questions:*

- *What does the recurring image of gun smoke tell us about Palmer's anxiety?*

- *Why does Palmer feel compelled to ignore Dorothy or tease her in public when privately he holds much respect for her?*

- *Even though most 10-year-olds in his town consider it an honor to be a wringer, why does Palmer abhor this tradition?*

Susan is excited about her thought-provoking questions. She administers the test and is greatly disappointed in the responses. Frustrated, she takes her assessment and student samples to her graduate class. The group finds her assessment well aligned with the stan-dards. They are "right on target" with the enduring learning she was hoping for.

"Why did they do so poorly?" Susan asks her classmates. "I am very disappointed. You should have heard the discussion. They summarized some of the chapters and para-phrased the others. We found text-to-self connections. I really thought this would be a wonderful representation of what they had learned."

The instructor of Susan's class led the entire group in a discovery process. The concept of mismatching instruction and assessment was loosely defined. Then the teachers looked carefully at the vocabulary in her questions. When asked whether she had used the words *compelling, abhors,* and *recurring,* Susan couldn't remember. She knew the concepts had been covered, but she wondered whether she had used a more sophisticated vocabulary because she was bringing the assessment to be reviewed by her peers.

It is quite possible that we create an assessment using vocabulary that we use naturally; we assume others use it as well. The lack of understanding what the questions were asking affected the student responses. Susan defined some of the words for individual students but did not make the connections for the entire class.

Mental Note: Be sure to use vocabulary words that you know your students are familiar with for your assessments.

Levels of Complexity

Sousa (2003) differentiates between levels of difficulty and levels of complexity. *Complexity* refers to the type of thought processes used to handle information and problems. *Difficulty* is the amount of effort needed within a level of complexity. Using the new Bloom's taxonomy (Anderson et al., 2001), *complexity* may be defined as the levels of thinking involved. The more complex a task is, the higher the level of thinking required. The more difficult a task is, the more effort is used at a particular level of thinking (see Figure 7.2).

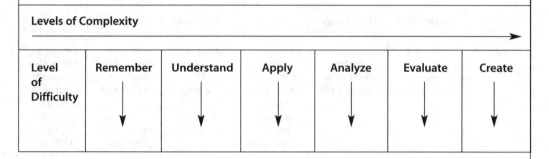

Figure 7.2
Bloom's Taxonomy in Determining Levels of Complexity and Difficulty in Thought Processes

Rehearsals and reviews must match the assessment in complexity. In general, rehearsals begin at the lower levels of the taxonomy for learning and then progress to more complex activities and exercises. By the final rehearsals and concluding review, be sure that the complexity level is equal to the assessment.

Using Susan's novel unit on *Wringer*, Figure 7.3 illustrates some possible questions with increasing complexity and added difficulty.

Mental Note: Students who encounter a complexity level beyond what has been rehearsed and reviewed may underperform on an assessment.

Transfer

The unit went really well. The students were attentive from the beginning when Mr. Perez introduced the Bill of Rights by showing a clip from the movie Born Yesterday. *Melanie Griffith's character learns the amendments by writing a song to the tune of "On the First Day of Christmas." The students loved it! He and the students wrote their own song to the tune and included only the Bill of Rights.*

Figure 7.3
Using the Novel Wringer to Illustrate Bloom's Revised Taxonomy

	Remember	Understand	Apply	Analyze	Evaluate	Create
Complexity	Who are the main characters in *Wringer*?	Why is Palmer upset about turning 10?	Compare the pigeon information in *Wringer* to that on one of the Internet sites listed.	What are the components of the tradition that Palmer has difficulty with?	Is Pigeon Day and the shooting of 5,000 birds a justified event to pay for the park's maintenance?	Design an alternative process that represents coming of age and will also fulfull the other results on Pigeon Day.
Difficulty	Describe their personalities.	Describe the reactions of two others in the book about turning 10.	Compare the pigeon information to three other sources, including one Internet site.	Take those components and prioritize them from the most offensive to the least offensive.	Include the amount of money gained and how it is specifically used.	Create an agenda for the process that can be used by the townspeople.

Mr. Perez also put the students in groups and had each group create a visual for an amendment. They had to present their visual and explain it. To be certain they knew the amendments, they created an "amendment dance." They had different movements for each amendment. For review, they played "Amendment Pursuit" modeled after Trivial Pursuit. Mr. Perez divided the class into two teams. He read the questions. As long as the team answered correctly, they could continue answering questions until they "Filled the Bill" by reaching 10 points. They also played a Password game using vocabulary from the amendments. This was to ensure their understanding of the wording of each amendment. The culminating activity was role-playing each amendment. The students also did this in groups.

The assessment Mr. Perez designed was a paper-and-pencil test. It contained multiple-choice, matching, true/false, and short-answer questions. The students did not do well.

The assessment for this unit was not a match for the instruction. Even though Mr. Perez had designed the assessment before he designed his instructional strategies, he did little to help the students store and practice information in the semantic pathway. They learned through the emotional pathway (role playing), through the procedural pathway (dance), and through the conditioned response pathway (song, games). At no time did he take the information that they stored and have them recode it in writing. His instruction and assessment were mismatched. His choices were to give more writing exercises to help the students get the information into this pathway or to use some of the activities as authentic assessments using appropriate scoring rubrics. To do the former, after each activity, the students could write a summary of what they did or do some peer teaching.

Because the brain tries to make sense of any information it is given, it takes the offered cues and begins searching. In this Bill of Rights unit, the students were searching a dead end. Perhaps if the assessment had referred them to the dance, song, and games, the students would have been able to access the information more easily. I am not saying that Mr. Perez should not have taught the unit this way. It was very effective to get the students involved. With just a few more steps in the plan, however, the assessment results would likely have been more impressive.

> **Mental Note: Retrieval will be faster if assessment matches the memory pathways used for instruction and assessment.**

Location! Location! Location!

I am in the gym with the cheerleaders. This is one of the few after-school practices we have in the large gymnasium where our games are played. The basketball coach will only give up this gym once every couple of weeks. The basketball teams are practicing in the small gym.

The girls have to rearrange themselves. They are much closer together for our other practices, and I am helping them center themselves. They have a new dance routine to practice for this Saturday's game as well as their cheers.

"Mrs. Sprenger, we've never done this dance in here," Christine announces frantically. "I always focused on the picture of the school while I was dancing. There's not a picture in here!"

"Don't worry, Christine, we'll be practicing every morning in here this week. Find another focal point and you'll be fine," I reply.

The squad is set. I turn to start the music when I see Keisha coming through the door. I had forgotten that I would give her a makeup quiz tonight after school.

She looks at me disapprovingly. "You aren't in your room. I've been waiting for you. If Mr. Bell hadn't seen me and told me where you are, I'd still be sitting there. This is the only night I can stay late and make up the quiz."

I apologize for my forgetfulness. I open my grade book and pull out a copy of the quiz. "Now, where can she take it?" I wonder to myself. "I don't want her back in the classroom without me. I'm afraid she'll look up the answers. It'll be too noisy in here." I check the coach's office, which is empty.

"Keisha, go into Mr. Blundy's office and close the door. You can take your quiz in there. If the music is too loud, let me know."

Keisha obeys. I go back to coaching the cheerleaders. Several minutes pass and Keisha appears before me.

"Finished already?" I ask. "Or is the noise bothering you?"

"It's not the noise, Mrs. Sprenger. It's the office. I can't think in there. I can't remember anything. I need to be in your room. I need my desk, and I need to see your chalkboard."

"There's nothing on the chalkboard, Keisha," I reply. "There are no answers there."

"They come into my head when I look at it. That's how I take all my tests," she insists.

I left the cheerleaders and took Keisha to my room. It wasn't fun or easy, but I ran back and forth between my two responsibilities. Mr. Blundy came into the gym and offered to keep an eye on the cheerleaders. Keisha finished her quiz quickly. She did very well.

I was fascinated with Keisha's comments. I started observing students taking tests in my room. My "action" research was compelling. I copied my class lists and started keeping some records of what students did when they were taking tests, quizzes, writing essays, and doing worksheets. I found that about 30 percent of the 8th graders became totally absorbed in what they were doing. I never saw them look around. About 40 percent glanced up occasionally but didn't seem to be looking at anything in particular. Another 15 to 20 percent looked at the chalkboard or at me every so often. But 5 to 10 percent of my students had to look at the chalkboard, the overhead screen, the bulletin board, or me every few minutes! Keisha was one of them.

The research on this phenomenon is persuasive. As far back as 1690, John Locke described a case of a young man who learned to dance in a room with an old trunk. He found that he could not remember dance steps without the presence of that trunk (Baddeley, 1999). As far as testing is concerned, it appears that recognition tests, which provide a certain number of cues, do not rely on the environment as much as recall tests do.

Two years ago, I had the opportunity to see this phenomenon played out in a state testing situation. A principal in a nearby community called me, very concerned about his school's writing test results. He wanted me to work with the teachers. I asked to see copies of the students' essays from the state assessment, and he was able to acquire some. All it took was for me to see that the students wrote insufficiently. The state did not have enough writing on each essay for them to know whether they could meet the standards.

"Where did these students take this test?" I asked the principal and the teachers. As someone pulled out the testing schedule, the 8th grade teacher started nodding his head. "They took the test in their homerooms. So some of them were with social studies teachers, some with science teachers, and some with math teachers," he announced. "Only my homeroom class was with me. I teach writing to 5th through 8th grades."

Examining the test scores of those students who happened to be in the language arts classroom, I could easily reach some interesting conclusions. Many more of the students who were writing in their writing classroom met or exceeded the standards. They simply wrote more. The environment and the presence of their writing teacher helped them connect to the writing expectations for an adequate essay. The other content area teachers did not expect extensive essays in their subjects, so the students wrote shorter pieces.

This experience led us to a discussion about expectations and common vocabulary. Why this experience occurred this particular year with these students, no one could say for certain. Perhaps the schedules had been different in the past. Perhaps these students were more sensitive to their environment.

As I travel and share this information with administrators and teachers, I ask them to consider the possibilities. We would assume with the proper amount of rehearsal and review, transfer would not be an issue. In most cases, it is not. But for some students, transfer may take more time. The consolidation of semantic memory is different for all of us. As Eichenbaum (2003) suggests, we take the episodes and extract the meaning that becomes a solid semantic memory. Because of differing brain development, attention, motivation, and experiences, I believe it behooves us to offer students every opportunity to perform well in a situation with such high stakes for us all.

Mental Note: Students who learn information in one location may retrieve it more readily in the same location.

Assessment Methods and Retrieval

It is important to review the two major types of assessment. *Formative* assessment is generally used within the classroom as a form of feedback to improve and increase learning. This may include paper-and-pencil tests, personal communication, performances, and portfolios. *Summative* assessment is a measurement of what students have learned at a certain period in time and may include a unit or chapter test and state or national achievement tests. All of these assessments should be aligned with the state or national goals. For the purpose of transfer, these assessments should focus on more than factual information. Conceptual understanding should be the main focus of the assessments (Bransford, Brown, & Cocking, 1999).

Performance Assessment

When students demonstrate what they know through a performance, retrieval is dependent on the type of performance assessment. Danielson (2002) describes two types: spontaneous and structured. A *spontaneous* performance may be through informal observation of the student during the rehearsal stage of learning. Anecdotal records may be kept, and rubrics may be used as well. The question is whether this type of assessment is graded. In *How to Grade for Learning*, O'Connor (1999) contends that a student's most recent effort should receive a grade, not the trials to reach that level. He also believes that we should be discussing the grading methodology with the students when we begin a new unit of study.

Structured authentic assessment is set up with the student prior to the performance. The students should have a rubric to guide them so they know exactly how they will be evaluated. Using these circumstances, students are well prepared, and retrieval is not normally an issue. Keep in mind, however, that performance anxiety, like test anxiety, can be a strong factor in how well the information necessary to perform is retrieved. If the student is performing for the class, public speaking may be an issue. Because offering students choices may lower stress levels, allowing them to pick the mode of performance assessment may alleviate some stress. Those terribly uncomfortable with an oral presentation may choose an essay, videotape, or some other product as a way to demonstrate their knowledge.

Traditional Tests

Paper-and-pencil tests usually require that the student work independently. There are also time limits, and usually outside resources, such as notes, cannot be used. In other words, the retrieval cues included on the assessment must be enough to trigger facts, concepts, and procedures. Therefore, it is imperative to use the right format to ascertain the information that is required. For instance, a constructed response test, such as an essay test, may be a better way to evaluate a student's ability to use the higher-level thinking skills of analyzing, applying, and evaluating. Different formats may be more suitable for factual knowledge, procedural knowledge, and conceptual knowledge (Stiggins, 2001; Danielson, 2002).

Selected response tests include multiple-choice, matching, and true/false questions. These are best at measuring a student's ability to retrieve facts and isolated concepts, although it is possible to construct a selected response test to determine if a student can analyze, apply, and evaluate.

Constructed response tests require that a student construct his own answers rather than choose a correct answer. These consist of fill-in-the-blank tests and essays. This type of test can measure larger conceptual understandings, problem solving, and higher-level processes.

> **Mental Note: Choosing the appropriate assessment may make the difference between successful and unsuccessful retrieval.**

When Retrieval Fails

If you have followed the seven steps, what do you do if there are students who still can't retrieve the information and understandings you expect? Several factors need to be checked along the way in every unit.

1. Did you step back? Did you begin with the end in mind? If you created your assessment based on the expectations, enduring understandings, and essential questions, then your students will have fewer retrieval problems. We sometimes have a tendency to change directions as we proceed through a unit. Continually connect what you are teaching to the first five Es: expectations, enduring learning, essential questions, evidence, and evaluation.

2. Are your students reflecting throughout the unit? Are you battling time and as a result skimping on reflection time? Check your reflection habits. Our curricula are accused of being a mile wide and an inch deep. *Give your students the opportunity to make deep connections through reflections.*

3. Are you providing enough reinforcement? Some research has found that the most powerful effect on student achievement is instructional reinforcement (Cotton, 2000). Check to see whether you are providing the feedback your students need to correct misconceptions and strengthen memory connections. Make use of peer evaluations and computer-based instructional reinforcement that provide immediate feedback.

4. Are you varying your rehearsal strategies to meet diverse needs? The need for differentiation is great. Check your rehearsal strategies for various modes of learning. If you find you must reteach, try rehearsals that meet needs you may not have met the first time around. Make the most of student strengths and guide them through their weaknesses.

5. Are you spacing your reviews appropriately? Check back to the chart in chapter 6 on spacing reviews. Make sure you are including reviews throughout the unit. If you are suspicious of student understanding, insert another review before moving on.

6. Reflect on your teaching experience. I don't know if I ever felt that I had executed the ideal unit. There was always something I learned as I taught, and there were always changes made each time. The only way to improve is to reflect and make adjustments. Forgive yourself if you have to reteach and reassess. Researchers have found that reteaching is critical for the students who require it to master learning material (Cotton, 2000).

Retrieval's Effect on Memory

It is the recovery of long-term memories in working memory that allows us to make new connections. Conceptual understandings and procedural understandings can then be reapplied in new and unusual circumstances. According to Squire and Kandel (1999), when material is well learned initially, forgetting occurs gradually. Memory works by extracting the meaning of what we encounter. From the many rehearsals and reviews, memory is established but later can be modified by new information and from the rehearsal process itself. Memory also can be distorted by how it is examined in a retrieval test.

Each time we retrieve memories, we reconstruct them and review them. If we have had the rehearsal strategies that have allowed us to rework the memories in a different way using higher-level thinking processes, we can build on those experiences and apply the information again in similar situations.

Retrieval may depend on many factors: the number of rehearsals, the spacing of reviews, the depth of understanding, the time for reflection, and the type and amount of reinforcement.

Reflection

1. The ability to retrieve information quickly and easily offers students a feeling of self-confidence. How do you reinforce these feelings in every student in your classroom?

2. Some students are naturally slow processors and slow retrievers. What do you do in your classroom to provide them with the optimal environment for assessment and retrieval?

3. A constant reminder: Does what you are accepting as evidence that your students have enduring understanding match your instructional strategies?

8

Realization

> It is perhaps self-evident that more effective teachers use more effective instructional strategies. It is probably also true that effective teachers have more instructional strategies at their disposal.
>
> —*Robert Marzano*, What Works in Schools

Carolyn is teaching writing again this year. She has 7th graders, so this is not a testing year for writing. She creates a Writer's Workshop for her students. She knows that writing is a process, and through the workshop the students will clearly see their writing change. Through different levels of group work and conferencing, she will take the opportunity to help them grow as writers. She has created her own rubrics through the years, and assessing student writing is second nature to Carolyn.

The new principal enters her room one day and hands Carolyn a flyer from the State Board of Education. It describes a workshop on writing and using the state rubric. He asks that she attend with several other language arts teachers.

The day of the workshop, she is bowled over. Her rubric and the state's do not match. She didn't know how many areas she was missing that the state thought important enough to be assessing. Because she was teaching in between-testing years, no one had put a lot of pressure on her. She knew her students progressed well in writing according to her standards. As the day wore on, it became clear that there were many things she didn't know.

Carolyn returns to her classroom the following day. In her hands she holds the state rubric and many handouts explaining each characteristic. Although she has the information, applying it seems like a monumental task. As she distributes the rubrics to the students and starts explaining, she begins to see the similarities to her own rubric. She also begins to make connections to what they have been doing in Writer's Workshop to the state standards. It takes many weeks, but finally it all falls into place. Her expectations for writing have changed. The targets for her students clearly change, and through a lot of experiences, her new learning becomes her new habits for teaching writing.

We have all had the experience of going from the awkward realization that we don't know anything to a feeling of competence. I was in high school the first time I heard the following: Freshmen don't know and don't know they don't know. Sophomores don't know and know they don't know. Juniors know and don't know they know. Seniors know and know they know.

And so it is with educators and other professionals. Before we are exposed to learning models and strategies that are scientifically based, we don't know. When the exposure begins, we realize how much we don't know. As we begin the process of learning through professional development, but before we actually try things out in the classroom, we don't know that we know. Then through actual classroom practice, we know. We develop a level of proficiency.

Summing Up the Seven Steps

Repetition is good for the brain. At least, that's what I tell my children when they tell me that I'm repeating myself! A short summary of each step follows. It is a reminder of the key points involved in teaching for memory.

Step 1: Reach

Your attention and motivational skills may not need an "extreme makeover." Many of your current unit plans may just need some tweaking. We need to remember that novelty is appealing to our students. In particular, adolescents respond well to both novelty and emotion (Feinstein, 2004). In chapter 1 you learned that the following might be helpful in reaching students and providing the first step toward long-term retention and transfer, getting information into sensory memory:

- Attention
- Motivation
- Emotion
- Meaning
- Relationships
- Novelty
- Advance organizers
- Relevancy

Mental Note: If you can't reach 'em, you can't teach 'em!

Step 2: Reflect

Offering students the opportunity to make connections requires that we give them some time. This step reminds us that educators need to be aware of wait time, focus time, and reflection time. Reflection allows students to search their memories for prior knowledge that they may have about the topic. By manipulating the new information in working memory, they connect the new information with older, long-term memories. This allows them to find a "hook" to hang new information on. The Seven Habits of Highly Reflective Classrooms were offered as suggestions:

1. Question
2. Visualize
3. Journal
4. Thinking directives
5. PMI
6. Collaborate
7. Four-corner reflection

Mental Note: Reflection is not a luxury; it's a necessity.

Step 3: Recode

While information is still in working memory, students must have the opportunity to put it in their own words. Research suggests that we remember better what we have produced. If our students can generate their own explanation of the concept, then it will be time to put the information into long-term storage. If the information is not clear to the student, the teacher can clear up any misconceptions or reteach. This is an opportunity to employ scientifically based research to help our students achieve. The following strategies are recommended for recoding:

- Interpreting
- Exemplifying
- Classifying
- Summarizing
- Inferring
- Comparing
- Explaining
- Using nonlinguistic representations

 Mental Note: Self-generated material is better remembered.

Step 4: Reinforce

At this step in the process, we let students know whether they understand the facts, concepts, or procedures. By assessing their recoding attempt without grading it and giving appropriate feedback, we can clear up misconceptions. The three types of feedback used in step 4 include:

- Motivational feedback,
- Informational feedback, and
- Developmental feedback.

Mental Note: Feedback is vital to learning.

Step 5: Rehearse

Once students can put concepts, facts, and procedures into their own words accurately, it is time to begin to transfer it to long-term memory. There are five memory pathways, various learning styles, and multiple intelligences approaches to use. Rote rehearsal is useful for some facts, but elaborative rehearsal provides more meaning. Multiple rehearsals are necessary. The accurate recoding only set up a network of neurons in their brains. It has not been practiced, so it will not become a permanent memory without some repetition and manipulation. This step takes the information from working memory and places it throughout the brain so it can be more easily accessed.

Concepts to keep in mind from this step include the following:

- Rote rehearsal
- Elaborative rehearsal
- Sleep
- Spacing
- Homework and practice
- Multiple pathways
- Multiple episodes

Mental Note: We remember better if we more fully process new subject matter.

Step 6: Review

Whereas rehearsal puts information in long-term memory, review presents the opportunity to retrieve that information and manipulate it in working memory. The products of the manipulation can then be returned to long-term memory. Timing of review is important. It is necessary to space reviews closely at first and then farther apart. The following points need to be considered:

- Match the review to instruction and assessment.
- Check for accuracy of the memory.
- Give students the conditions to use higher-level thinking skills to analyze, evaluate, and possibly create alternative ways to use the knowledge.
- Strengthen the existing networks.
- For high-stakes testing, practice similar questions under similar conditions.
- Avoid cramming.

Mental Note: Without review, most information will be lost from memory.

Step 7: Retrieve

The ability to access long-term memories, bring them into the working memory process, and solve problems is the culmination of the memory process. Retrieval is most successful when the context and the cues that were present when the material was first learned are the same as the context and the cues that are present later when making an attempt to recall. The following concepts are covered in this step:

- Type of assessment
- Specific cues
- Recognition techniques
- Recall strategies
- Stress

| Mental Note: Memory retrieval may be dependent on cues. | |

Metacognition

Through the step-by-step process, students begin to discover how they learn and remember. By doing so, they naturally begin to reflect while learning and become metacognitive. Metacognition involves two phases. The first is knowledge about cognition or thinking about our thinking. The second is monitoring and regulating cognitive processes (Anderson et al., 2001). Recent research suggests that both of these phases play a vital role in student learning (Bransford et al., 1999).

The seven steps outlined in this book assist in both phases. I have stressed the importance of reflection, not only as step 2 but also as a process to be implemented after each step, each rehearsal, and each review. The practice of reflecting about what we know, what we don't know, and how best to learn what we don't know will lead us to processing information at the appropriate level or step. Our goal is to get memories solidified for long-term storage and transfer. The steps take us through the memory processes, and when we know which step we are on or where in memory the facts, concepts, and procedures are, then we can proceed from that step to the next. (See Figure 8.1 for a review of the seven steps.)

During the first week of school, I teach my students about how the brain learns and remembers. I offer them the steps to long-term memory and share mnemonic devices. I test their memories with simple tests to make them feel successful. As we start each unit, I make sure the targets are clear and explain the process that we will go through to get the new facts, concepts, and procedures into long-term memory. I ask them to think about their thinking.

Often we ask others, "What are you thinking?" This question may be asked in a sarcastic manner, or it may be a true inquiry. The question I like to ask is "How are you thinking?" I want my students to be aware of their thinking processes and be able to articulate them. Once they can explain how they are thinking, they will begin to question themselves and metacognition and metacognitive control take place.

Figure 8.1
The Seven Steps to Remembering

Step	Characteristics	Memory Process
1. Reach	Attention Motivation Emotion Learning styles	Sensory > Immediate
2. Reflect	Question Collaborate Visualize	Immediate > Working
3. Recode	Self-generate Symbolize Dialogue	Working
4. Reinforce	Feedback Reteach Reinvent	Working Emotional
5. Rehearse	Repeat Rote Elaborative Spacing	Working > Long-term
6. Review	Matching instruction Anticipated problems Unanticipated problems	Long-term > Working > Long-term
7. Retrieve	Assessment Cues Stress/test anxiety	Long-term > Working Emotional Memory

I have developed an if-then chart to help assess where a student is in the memory process and which step to go to next (Figure 8.2). Students can also use this chart to self-assess. Once they truly know their own memory processes and strengths, they will be able to figure out what they need to do next.

> **Mental Note: Metacognition and metacognitive control occur through asking oneself, "How am I thinking?"**

Figure 8.2
An If-Then Chart to Assess Students' Needs

If a student cannot recognize the material ...	If a student cannot put the facts, concept, or procedure in his own words but can repeat yours ...	If a student can't recall during a review ...	If a student cannot recall on a practice quiz ...	If a student can recognize but not recall ...	If a student can recode but has difficulty with rehearsals ...	If a student can apply, analyze, and evaluate ...
Go back to step 1, reach.	Go back to step 2, reflect.	Go back to step 3, recode.	Give a recognition quiz.	Go back to step 3, recode, and try a new recoding process.	Go back to step 4, re-inforcement, and offer developmental feedback.	Go to step 5, rehearsal, and add creativity or another level of complexity; or review, assess and move on.

Teacher Exposure to Current Research

A teacher's knowledge level and skill level can drastically affect student achievement (Darling-Hammond, 1997). Limitations occur when the teacher is restricted by her own familiarity with content. Other studies have found that teacher expectations enhance or worsen student achievement (Danielson, 2002). Those expectations will be higher when teachers are more expert in their fields and have more strategies at hand. Teaching for understanding will be encouraged.

Many times teachers say, "I don't care about the why. Just tell me what to do." I feel strongly that the why is what keeps us doing the important things. Knowing that identifying similarities and differences can raise achievement 45 percentile points (Marzano, Pickering, & Pollack, 2001) is the reason that I continually find and use strategies to teach it.

All educators need to be aware of the scientifically based research on teaching strategies as well as the latest cognitive science research on how the brain learns and remembers. Peterson (2000) has said that memory research is one area of neuroscience that can be applied in the classroom.

According to Schenck (2000), 75 percent of a student's performance is based on what occurs prior to review and assessment. Motivation, attention, recoding, reinforcement, and rehearsals make up three-quarters of a student's grade. The other 25 percent is a combination of the reviews and the assessment itself.

Educators must have access to current studies and publications that will enhance their ability to encourage students' memories and understandings. As a classroom teacher, you become an expert. With the proper background knowledge, you will be able to select the appropriate tools to engage your students and enhance their understandings. Experimental studies will provide overviews and advice based on current trends. Case studies will offer new instructional and assessment methods to be considered. A multiple-year cross-sectional study helps separate performance that is unique to a specific cohort (i.e., a group of students in a single grade) from performance that is related to teaching and other factors. Other studies, such as correlational studies, provide information about how variables affect each other.

Professional development for teachers indicates that a school district is interested not only in raising student achievement but also in providing teachers with the tools they need. It is not a sign that teachers need "fixing." Rather, it is an indication that the learning community is always open to learning more and better ways to assist in student understanding. One-shot professional development may offer a few strategies to use on Monday, but ongoing training with feedback will have a greater impact on changing old habits and developing more effective strategies that will be used in an automatic fashion. As teachers know, when the going gets tough, it is easy to fall back into old reliable habits—even if they are ineffective. Just as our students need rehearsal and feedback to gain long-term understanding, so do we. A final point that must never be underestimated is that most of the time, we do know that we don't know, and our voices must be considered when it comes to what professional development is needed.

> **Mental Note: Teachers should be exposed to current scientific research about how the brain learns, remembers, and transfers.**

Retention or Retention?

If a student is unable to retain the necessary information to demonstrate her ability to meet or exceed state or national standards, should the student be retained? In this age of accountability, is it simply a matter of retention or retention? The effectiveness of retaining students is questionable. According to an ASCD Research Brief (2004) on "Attention and Student Achievement," "In this era of accountability, many school systems have begun taking a harder line with regard to promotion policy, retaining students who do not make sufficient academic progress—particularly in reading and math." Yet, reading researcher Sally Shaywitz (2003) says, "Above all, do not keep the child back a year in school . . . retention is not effective." According to her research, students who are not retained are better off academically and emotionally.

Reading specialist Debra Johnson (2001) completed a review of current literature on the topic of social promotion and retention. She found that retention affects behavior, attitude, and attendance. Current literature and current practice suggests that five strategies may serve as alternatives to retention or social promotion:

- **Intensify learning.** Develop rigorous standards, clear targets, and a rich curriculum; provide knowledgeable and skilled teachers; and create meaningful learning experiences.

- **Ensure skilled teachers by providing professional development.** Ongoing, meaningful professional development can greatly impact student achievement.

- **Expand learning options.** Use ongoing assessment, differentiation, and brain-based teaching.

- **Assess to inform.** Use both formative and summative assessment as feedback for students and teachers.

- **Intervene early.** Offer increased instructional time, and provide alternate methods of learning.

The purpose of this book is retention—retaining meaningful information that will raise student achievement and avoid the likelihood of holding students back a grade. The emotional impact of repeating grades can be traumatic. According to Sevener (1990), children view the thought of flunking a grade to be almost as stressful as the death of a parent or blindness. Shared expectations by students and teachers, reflection, rehearsal, reinforcement, and review can provide pertinent information to all stakeholders. Promoting students should be based on classroom assessment as well as high-stakes testing. Memory retention and transfer are our goals.

Success Breeds Success, for Students and Teachers

As our students retain more, they will be convinced that their memories are good and will put forth the effort to continue learning. I suggest that you ask your students to describe how they have learned something that they enjoy and in which they excel. Show them how their learning follows a pattern. As students climb the steps toward long-term memory, the events build upon one another. Show success with each step by using a reinforcement plan that includes informational feedback in a visual representation. Let your students see and feel their successes.

You will also feel successful as your students achieve. A success cycle will form as they become more eager to learn and you become more comfortable with the learning and memory process. It will become easier to pinpoint problem areas for each student and overcome them.

I encourage you to take the first step.

Reflection

1. As your own learning curve goes up through the seven steps, think about your own thinking. What steps in the process are easiest for you? Where can you find help for a difficult step?

2. How familiar are you with current research? Perhaps you can begin a book study group at your school.

3. Do you have a voice in your own professional development? Consider your needs and compare them with those of your colleagues.

4. Is teacher turnover a problem in your school? What kind of teacher mentoring is available in your district?

5. Could you be part of a teacher peer group or learning team to support each other in aligning instruction to the standards and teaching for memory to ensure success for more students?

A

Brain Briefing

This appendix reviews some basic structures and functions in the brain to help you understand the memory process.

Lobes of the Brain

There are four major lobes of the brain (Figure A.1). The brain is divided into a left and a right hemisphere, and each hemisphere contains its own side of the lobes. The left hemisphere is associated with details, whereas the right tends to get the "big picture." Because memories are stored in different areas of the brain, an understanding of the functions and locations of each is desirable.

Parietal. The parietal lobes are located toward the back of the top of your head. Here we find the ability to process sensory stimuli, spatial awareness, and some problem solving.

Occipital. The occipital lobes are located in the middle of the back of the brain. They process visual stimuli. Memories of objects, people, and so forth, are kept here to provide meaning to new information and make sense of the visual world.

Figure A.1
The Four Major Lobes of the Brain, Wernicke's Area, and Broca's Area

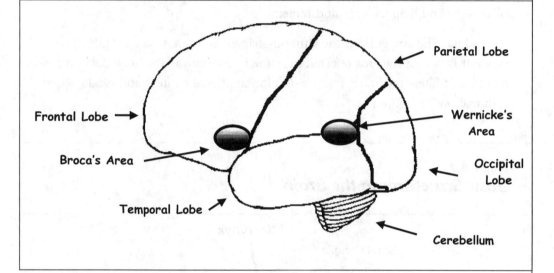

Temporal. The temporal lobes are located on the sides of your head above your ears. They are responsible for auditory information, some memory, and some speech.

Frontal. The frontal lobes are located toward the front of the top of your head and behind your forehead. This large area of the brain is responsible for executive functions such as working memory, higher-level thinking, future planning, decision making, and making choices.

Mental Note: Memories are dispersed throughout the lobes of the brain.

Structures

Within the brain are many structures with various functions relating to memory (Figures A.1 and A.2). Even though their purposes appear to be specific to them, the brain is really a system of systems. Many brain areas work together to accomplish tasks and help us learn and remember.

Amygdala. The amygdala is the almond-shaped structure in the middle of the brain. It is part of the area referred to as the *limbic system*. The amygdala processes emotion. It filters incoming information for emotional content and catalogs that information for future use.

Figure A.2
Basic Structures in the Brain

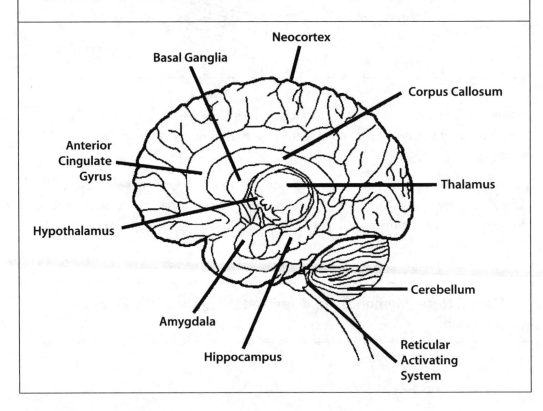

Anterior cingulate. This structure, located in the frontal lobe, is associated with attention, emotion, motivation, and memory.

Basal ganglia. Part of the reward system in the brain, these structures deep within the cortex are also responsible for some of our memories. Evidence points to the basal ganglia as the primary site for learning sequential information (Quartz & Sejnowski, 2002).

Broca's area. Located just behind the left temple, this area is associated with speech production, including vocabulary, syntax, and grammar (expressive language).

Cerebellum. The "little brain" is located beneath the occipital lobes in the back of the brain. Long thought to only be associated with balance, new research shows that this structure plays an important role in navigating movement and thought processes (Giedd, 2002).

Hippocampus. Close to the amygdala lies the hippocampus. Also a limbic structure, located deep in the temporal lobe, the hippocampus processes incoming information that is factual. This is a critical structure involved in facilitating the short-term to long-term memory process.

Neocortex. The top layer of the brain, the neocortex is one-fourth to one-eighth of an inch thick. It is here that many of our memories are stored in the different lobes.

Nucleus accumbens. An important structure associated with the reward system. It is located in the middle of the brain and is strongly networked to the amygdala.

Reticular activating system. This structure, located at the base of the brain, controls arousal. It connects the frontal lobes, limbic system, brainstem, and sense organs. The hippocampus also communicates with the reticular activating system. If this system overarouses us, the hippocampus can compare the information with the past and supervise events as either novel or commonplace (Ratey, 2001).

Thalamus. The thalamus is located in the middle of the brain and is sometimes considered part of the limbic system. This vital structure filters all incoming sensory information and relays it to the proper association area of each lobe.

Wernicke's area. Located in the left hemisphere, this region is thought to be responsible for language comprehension (receptive language).

> **Mental Note: Many structures are involved in storage and retrieval of memories.**

The Information Highway

All sensory information enters our brain through the brain stem, except for the sense of smell, which is directly processed into the limbic system. This is why smells bring back powerful memories—they connect immediately to the amygdala and hippocampus.

The first filtering structure in the brain is the reticular activating system. It sifts through the information to determine what stimuli to focus on. How does it know what to focus on? There are some basics that it follows: Survival is first and foremost (ever try to concentrate when you're hungry?), novelty is next, and then comes the power of choice. We can attend to anything that we want to attend to. As I sit here typing on my keyboard, until I concentrate on how the keys feel against my fingers, that bit of information is overlooked. If there were syrup on one of the keys, my brain would instantly focus on this novel (and sticky!) experience. Our awareness of the purpose of this system will become more important when we discuss attention.

From the reticular activating system, information flows to the thalamus. Like the old switchboard operators, the thalamus connects the information with its primary destination: visual information is directed to the occipital lobe, auditory information to the temporal lobe, and so forth. Each of these lobes has its own *association cortex* where the information is identified and associated with previous knowledge. Once this process is complete, the information returns to the middle of the brain where the hippocampus and the amygdala can filter it. If the information is factual, the hippocampus will hold it until it can be stored in long-term memory in the neocortex; it also catalogs it to make it possible to access. If it is emotional content, the amygdala will do the same. After information is catalogued, it is redistributed to the sensory areas for long-term storage.

Cells

The approximately three pounds of brain tissue that we each possess contains several different kinds of brain cells. About 10 percent of the mass consists of cells called *neurons* (Figure A.3). These cells learn and store memories. They connect to each other by means of an electrochemical bond and form networks. These networks are activated and store our memories.

A neuron has formations called *dendrites*. These could be compared to branches on a tree. The dendrites receive information from other neurons. That information or message attaches itself to a receptor site on the dendrite. The message goes to the *cell body* and down the structure called the *axon*, which could be compared to the trunk of a tree. Each neuron has only one axon but it can have

Figure A.3
The Neuron

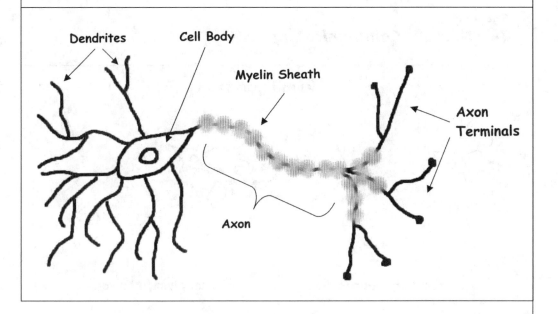

thousands of dendrites. The axon will grow *terminals* (roots) in order to send multiple messages. When the message leaves the axon, it is in the form of a chemical, a *neurotransmitter*. This chemical crosses a space called a *synapse* and attaches itself to the dendrite of the next neuron.

When neurons communicate, they are said to "fire" (Figure A.4). Although electrical activity is always occurring in the brain—that is, neurons are usually emitting low levels of electrical activity—when neurons are not firing rhythmically and purposefully, they are said to be "at rest." Neurons that fire together in a pattern are called *neural networks*. These networks form the patterns and programs in our brains. So, a memory requires a network of neurons to fire. You have stored millions of these networks.

The other 90 percent of the brain cells are called *glial cells*. *Glial* means "glue," and it describes many of the functions of these cells. They perform duties that nurture the neurons. Providing physical and nutritional support, glial cells hold

Figure A.4
Two Neurons Communicating

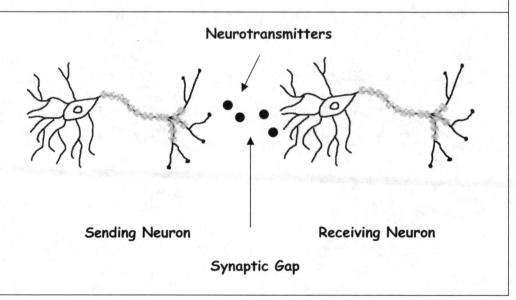

Neurotransmitters

Sending Neuron   Receiving Neuron

Synaptic Gap

neurons in place, transport nutrients, and digest debris. Their assistance provides strong connections between neurons, and without them memory would be affected (Barres, 1997).

One particular type of glial cell insulates the neurons to speed up the transmission of messages within the networks. This insulation is called *myelin*. It is a white lipid that is distributed throughout the brain in a developmental fashion (Eliot, 1999). For instance, at birth, myelin has already developed in some brain areas such as those pertaining to hearing, some movement, and the sucking reflex. The last area of the brain to become "myelinated" is the prefrontal cortex, which is the frontal lobe area right behind the forehead. Once this is myelinated, decision making, future planning, and other higher-level functions become easier. This area, however, may not be completely coated with myelin until the 20s or 30s!

Chemicals

The process of neurons communicating and setting up networks is electrochemical. Within the neuron, the process is electrical, but between neurons chemicals run the show. There are dozens of these chemicals, called *neurotransmitters*, in the brain. For memory purposes, we will isolate a few of them.

Acetylcholine. This chemical is vital to getting information into long-term memory. The levels are significantly higher when we sleep, supporting the theory that memories are reinforced during some of the sleep stages.

Dopamine. Dopamine is a neurotransmitter with several purposes in the brain. Many receptors for dopamine are found in the basal ganglia, part of the reward system. It is this system that profoundly affects long-term decision making and memories that run our lives (Halber, 2003).

Endorphin. This neurotransmitter is usually associated with the "runner's high," a feeling of euphoria from putting forth physical energy. It is also a necessary contributor to learning and memory.

GABA (gamma-aminobutyric acid). This is a calming neurotransmitter that keeps the brain from being overstimulated. Low levels are associated with anxiety (Whitaker, 1999).

Glutamate. This stimulating neurotransmitter activates systems involved in learning and memory.

Norepinephrine. The brain requires norepinephrine to form new memories and to transfer them to long-term storage. It is the primary excitatory neurotransmitter needed for motivation, alertness, and concentration.

Serotonin. This is a calming neurotransmitter. Serotonin plays an important role in regulating memory and learning, as well as appetite and body temperature. Low serotonin levels produce insomnia and depression, aggressive behavior, and increased sensitivity to pain. In order to pay attention and make good decisions, a balance in this chemical is useful.

> **Mental Note: Memories are stored in networks of neurons that communicate chemically through neurotransmitters.**

Searching for Memory

Sensory Memory

All information enters our brains through one of our senses: taste, smell, sight, hearing, or touch. Sensory memories are fleeting. They last seconds or less—just long enough for our brains to recognize what we are experiencing. After the thalamus directs new content to the appropriate association cortex, it returns to the hippocampal area where the sensations are reunited into the complete incident. Attention to it will allow it to stay in the next memory process, immediate memory (Arden, 2002).

Immediate Memory

If we pay attention to the incoming sensory information, we can hold onto it for about 20 seconds. This memory process is sometimes referred to as *conscious memory* or *short-term memory*, but we really have two short-term memory processes, immediate and working.

This memory practice allows us to look up the number to a restaurant and hold that number in our minds long enough to get it dialed. If we are interrupted in the process, the number slips our mind, and we must look it up again. Immediate memory stores up to seven bits of information for those 20 or so seconds.

Active Working Memory

Taking information from immediate memory and working with it encompasses this memory process. Working memory provides the time and space to manipulate information that is needed for complex cognitive tasks (Baddeley, 1999). Increasing the capacity of working memory helps students perform better on standardized tests (Klein & Boals, 2001). Often long-term memories are brought into working memory to supply prior knowledge that may be associated with the new material. Working memory can hold information for hours, days, or even weeks. In order for information to make it to long-term memory, it must become meaningful in some way. In other words, connections have to be made in the brain between the new material and previously stored material.

In school, our students use working memory as they are solving math problems, answering essay questions, and reading stories and texts. They hold and manipulate pieces of information to create new ideas, formulate hypotheses, and solve problems.

Long-term Memory

Information that becomes a detailed representation in memory is considered a permanent memory. This type of memory is lasting. It occurs when networks in our brains are created and used often enough that activation occurs easily and the information can be retrieved.

What happens with brand-new information? What if there is no prior knowledge? This is a question I often am asked. New material can be stored in long-term memory through different pathways. Perhaps putting information to music or movement will help store it. Adding a strong emotional component may make the difference between forgetting and remembering. Sometimes pointing out similarities and differences between certain kinds of information can help make sense out of it and allow it to be stored.

To perform complex cognitive tasks, our students must maintain access to large amounts of knowledge. There are large demands on working memory during activities such as text comprehension and skilled performance, so that the usual representation of working memory involving just temporary storage must be extended to include working memory based on information previously stored in long-term memory. For example, a student reading a story must have access to previously mentioned characters and scenarios for proper references for pronouns. The student also needs contextual information to integrate logically information presented in the current sentence with the text previously read. Similarly, in mathematical calculations the student must maintain the results of transitional steps in memory (i.e., mental math problems). Long-term memory and working memory interact at these times.

Long-term memory can be separated into two types of memory: explicit and implicit. Then these types of memory can be further divided into specific kinds of memory (see Figure A.5).

Figure A.5
Functional Divisions of Long-term Memory

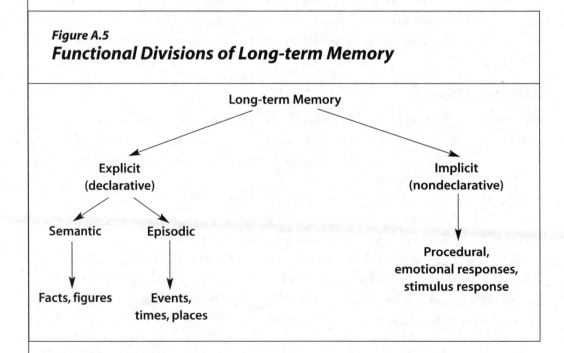

> **Mental Note: Memory must go through several different processes to become permanent.**

Explicit Memory

Explicit memory is exercised when performance on a task requires conscious remembrance of previous experience (Graf & Schacter, 1985). It may be easier to understand this type of memory if you think of it as *direct* memory (Baddeley, 1999). Explicit memory consists of long-term memories that are consciously learned. This includes semantic and episodic memory. Both are learned through the same brain structure, the hippocampus, yet they are very separate types of memory. The hippocampus appears to repeatedly play patterns of information, gradually training the appropriate area of cortex to acquire permanent memory.

The differences between episodic and semantic memory are notable for educators. According to Tulving (1999), *episodic* memory implies remembering, whereas *semantic* memory implies knowing. Remembering always involves knowing, but knowing does not necessarily imply remembering. We can use both of these memory pathways to help our students succeed and raise achievement levels. Both pathways can be influenced by multimodal experiences. They are each accessible through a variety of retrieval routes.

Because semantic and episodic memory both involve the knowledge of facts, both can be brought to mind, and both can be declared, they are sometimes called *declarative memory* (Bourtchouladze, 2002).

Episodic Memory

Tulving (1985) refers to episodic memory as *autonoetic*, which means knowing about yourself. This type of memory refers to locations and descriptions of events and people. Episodes, if you will, have a story effect—a beginning, a middle, and an end. They are memories that are distinct in time and space. We can consciously remember past experiences. Episodic memory is stored through the hippocampus. It catalogs these events, experiences, and locations.

A study of London cab drivers gives evidence of how we can change the brain and add memories. To become a London cabbie, one must study for two years.

Cabbies' brains were scanned at the start and end of this period, and the results showed the hippocampi of the drivers increased over the two years. With more experience driving, their brains continued to change (Thomas, 2000).

Episodic memory is context related. Results of studies show us that when we learn something in a specific location, we will recall it better in that same location (Baddeley, 1999).

Semantic Memory

Semantic memory is *noetic*, or knowing. Semantic memories are not necessarily time or space related but are context-free knowledge of facts, language, or concepts. They are also stored through the hippocampus. This structure is too small to store all of our semantic memories, so it feeds the information to the proper area of the neocortex. This process takes some time (and some sleep!). The hippocampus also catalogs the information so that the memory can be easily retrieved. Most researchers believe that at some point the hippocampus is not necessary to access the memory. Through a special process, memories become accessible without this pathway; however, it can take days, months, or even years for this to occur (Siegel, 1999).

Semantic memory is not learned all at once; it is learned through repetition. This is information that we learn; once it is learned, we generally forget how or when we learned it.

> **Mental Note: The educational system uses explicit memory most of the time.**

Implicit Memory

Implicit memory is sometimes referred to as *nondeclarative memory*. In contrast to intentional learning that is explicit, implicit learning is incidental or nonconscious. It is *indirect* learning (Baddeley, 1999). Some of these memories began explicitly but through repetition became implicit. In other words, we do something procedural like driving the car but do not consciously draw to mind the instructions for doing so. Besides procedural knowledge, implicit memory includes emotional responses, skills and habits, and stimulus responses.

Procedural Memory

This is our "know how" memory. It is timeless and does not involve conscious recollection. Although sometimes called *muscle memory*, procedural memory can be both motor and nonmotor (Levine, 2002). The basal ganglia and the cerebellum are involved in this type of memory.

Sequences that are repeated are stored in this memory pathway. They may be motor procedures, such as riding a bike and tying a shoe, or nonmotor procedures, such as telling a story from beginning to end and the sequence of the scientific method.

Saying "please" and "thank you" are habits that we acquired through learning the procedures of good manners.

Emotional Memory

If we look again at the amygdala in the middle of the brain, we can see how close it is to the thalamus. Some say that it is just one neuron away (Goleman, 1995). This implies that the emotional area of our brains receives and filters incoming information quickly—even before it has a chance to go up to the neocortex for higher-level thinking and recognition. Because of this, information that is not neutral will be examined and stored by the amygdala. The amygdala will react to emotional content without our conscious knowledge of it.

Stimulus Response

Considered a reflexive memory, the stimulus response is a response to a particular stimulus. It has been compared to the "hot stove" effect. Or, someone sneezes, and your response is "God bless you." When we teach students opposites, they often become "automatic" learning. I say, "Stop"; my students say, "Go." Flash cards and rap songs create this type of learning (Jensen, 1998).

> **Mental Note: Implicit memory may be more powerful and lasting than explicit memory.**

Graphic Organizers

Figure B.1
Venn Diagram

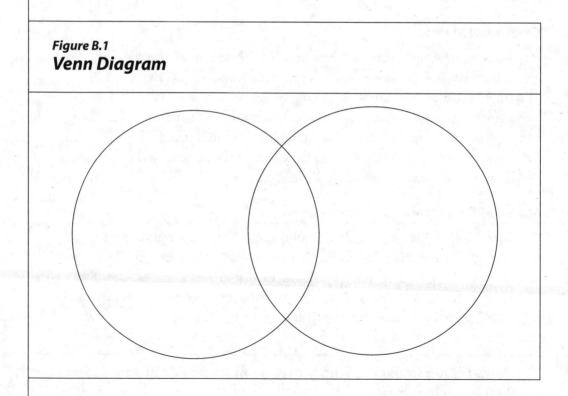

Figure B.2
Mind Map

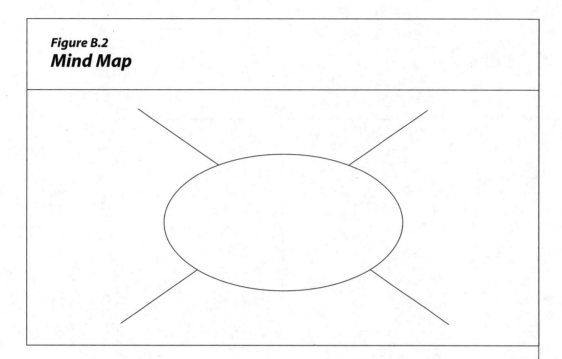

Figure B.3
KWHLU Chart

K	W	H	L	U

Adapted from Ogle (1986).

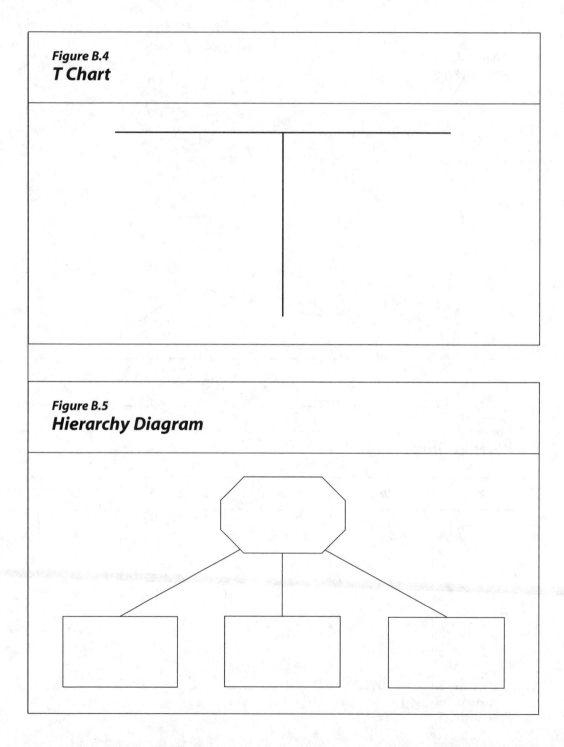

Figure B.4
T Chart

Figure B.5
Hierarchy Diagram

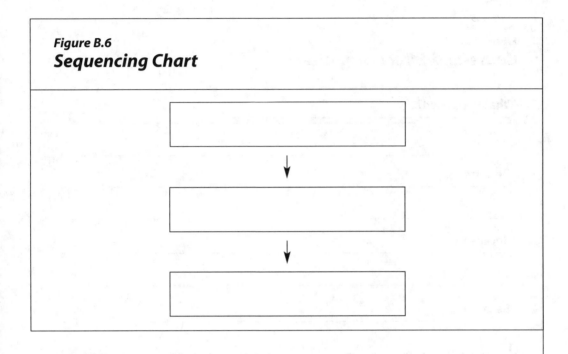

Figure B.6
Sequencing Chart

Figure B.7
PMI Chart

Plus	Minus	Interesting

Plus: What did you understand about the presentation?
Minus: What did you have trouble with? Dislike?
Interesting: What areas would you like to know more about?

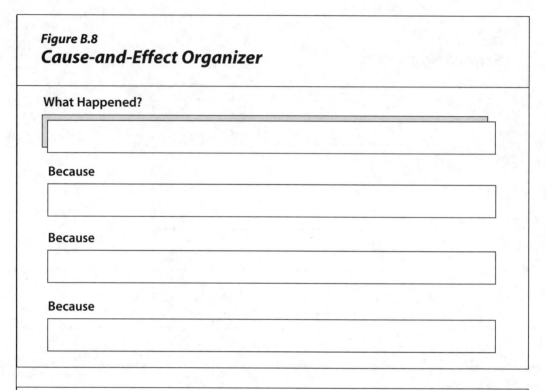

Figure B.8
Cause-and-Effect Organizer

What Happened?

Because

Because

Because

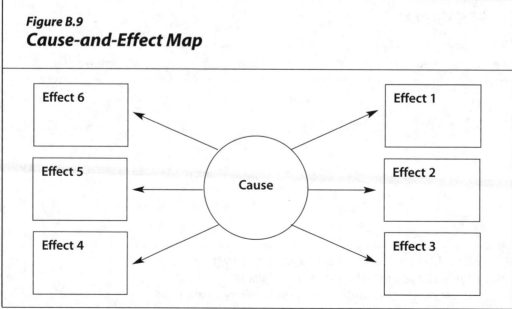

Figure B.9
Cause-and-Effect Map

Effect 6

Effect 1

Effect 5

Cause

Effect 2

Effect 4

Effect 3

Figure B.10
Cause-and-Effect Chain

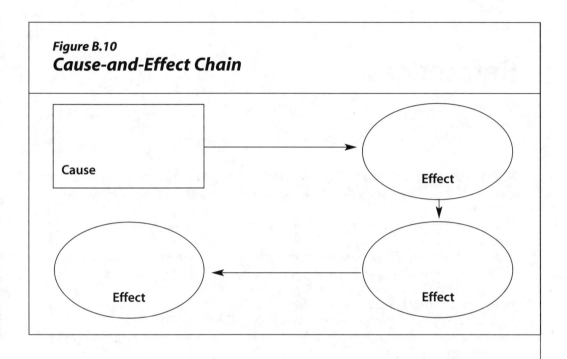

Figure B.11
Graphic Organizer for Exemplifying

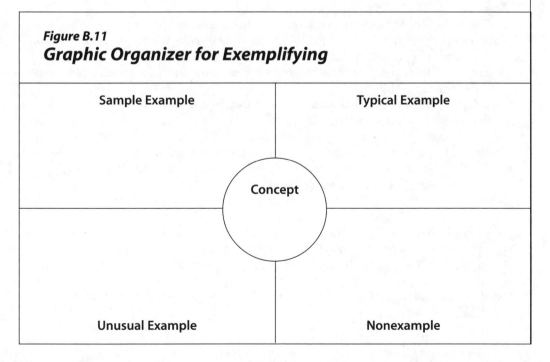

References

ACT, Inc. (2004). *Test preparation* [Online]. Available: http://www.act.org/aap/testprep/

American Heritage Dictionary of the English Language. (2000). 4th ed. Boston: Houghton Mifflin.

Anderson, J. R. (2000). *Learning and memory: An integrated approach* (2nd ed.). New York: Wiley.

Anderson, L., Krathwohl, D., Airasian, P., Cruikshank, K., Mayer, R., Pintrich, P., Raths, J., & Wittrock, M. (Eds.). (2001). *A taxonomy for learning, teaching, and assessing.* New York: Longman.

Andreason, N. (2001). *Brave new brain.* New York: Oxford University Press.

Arden, J. (2002). *Improving your memory for dummies.* New York: Wiley.

Arendal, L., & Mann, V. (2000) *Fast ForWord Reading: Why it works.* Berkeley, CA: Scientific Learning.

Armstrong, T. (1993). *Seven kinds of smart.* New York: Plume.

ASCD. (2001). *The brain and math* [Video series]. Alexandria, VA: Author.

ASCD Research Brief. (2004, May). Retention and student achievement. Vol. 2(11) [Online]. Available: http://www.ascd.org/publications/researchbrief/volume2/v2n11_link8.html

Atkins, S., & Murphy, K. (1993). Reflection: A review of the literature. *Journal of Advanced Nursing, 18*(8), 1188–1192.

Baddeley, A. (1999). *Essentials of human memory.* East Sussex, UK: Psychology Press.

Bangert-Drowns, R. L., Kulik, J. A., & Kulik, C.-L. (1983). Effects of coaching programs on achievement test performance. *Review of Educational Research, 53,* 571–585.

Barres, B. (1997). Lowly glia strengthen brain connections. Stanford University Press Release [Online]. Available: http://www.med.stanford.edu/center/communications/news_releases_html/1997/sepreleases/glial.html

Beidel, D. C., & Turner, S. M. (1999). Teaching study skills and test-taking strategies to elementary school students. *Behavior Modification, 23,* 630.

Blakeslee, S. (2000, April 30). Sleep on it may be a lesson worth heeding. *New York Times* [Online]. Available: http://www.jsonline.com/alive/news/apr00/sleep01043000.asp

Bloom, F., Beal M. F., & Kupfer, D. (Eds.). (2003). *The Dana guide to brain health.* New York: Dana.

Boud, D., Keough, R., & Walker, D. (1985). *Reflection: Turning experience into learning.* London: Kogan Page.

Bourtchouladze, R. (2002). *Memories are made of this*. London: Columbia University Press.

Bransford, J., Brown, A., & Cocking, R. (Eds.). (1999). *How people learn: Brain, mind, experience, and school*. Washington, DC: National Academy Press.

Brophy, J. (1987, October). Synthesis of research on strategies for motivating students to learn. *Educational Leadership*, 40–48.

Bruning, R. H., Schraw, G. J., & Ronning, R. (1999). *Cognitive psychology and instruction*. Upper Saddle River, NJ: Prentice-Hall.

Burke, K. (1999). *How to assess authentic learning* (3rd ed.). Arlington Heights, IL: SkyLight.

Burmark, L. (2002). *Visual literacy: Learn to see, see to learn*. Alexandria, VA: ASCD.

Burrows, D. (1995). The nurse teacher's role in the promotion of reflective practice. *Nurse Education Today, 15*(5), 346–350.

Butler, R. (1987). Task-involving and ego-involving properties of evaluation: Effects of different feedback conditions on motivational perceptions, interest and performance. *Journal of Educational Psychology, 79*(4), 474–482.

Buzan, T. (1974). *Use both sides of your brain*. London: Penguin Books.

Cahill, L. (2004). *Ten things every educator should know about the amygdala*. Presentation at the Winter Learning Brain Expo, San Diego, CA.

Caine, R., & Caine, G. (1994). *Making connections: teaching and the human brain*. Alexandria, VA: ASCD.

Carter, C., MacDonald, A., Ursu, S., Stenger, A., Ho Sohn, M., & Anderson, J. (2000, November). *How the brain gets ready to perform*. Paper presented at the 30th Annual Meeting of the Society of Neuroscience, New Orleans.

Carter, R. (1998). *Mapping the mind*. Los Angeles: University of California Press.

Casanova, U., & Berliner, D. (1986, February). Should students be made test-wise? *Instructor, 95*(6), 22–23.

Chapman, C., & King, R. (2000). *Test success*. Tucson, AZ: Zephyr.

Chappuis, S., & Stiggins, R. (2002, September). Classroom assessment for learning. *Educational Leadership, 60* (1), 40–43.

Ciardiello, A. (1998). Did you ask a good question today? Alternative cognitive and metacognitive strategies. *Journal of Adolescent & Adult Literacy, 42*, 210–219.

Cohen, J. (1999). *Educating minds and hearts*. Alexandria, VA: ASCD.

Colbert, B., & Knapp, P. (2000, October 18). *This sucks. You're stupid: Giving negative feedback*. Paper presented at the William Mitchell College of Law, Midwest Clinic Conference.

Comer, J. (2003). Transforming the lives of children. In M. Elias, H. Arnold, & C. Hussey (Eds.), *EQ + IQ = Best leadership practices*. Thousand Oaks, CA: Corwin.

Connellan, T. (2003). *Bringing out the best in others*. Austin, TX: Bard Press.

Cooke, V. (1991). *Writing across the curriculum: A faculty handbook*. Victoria, Canada: Centre for Curriculum and Professional Development.

Costa, A., & Kallick, B. (2000). Describing 16 habits of mind. Retrieved from http://www. habitsofmind.net/pdf/16HOM2.pdf

Cotton, K. (2000). *The schooling practices that matter most.* Alexandria, VA: ASCD.

Covey, S. (1989). *The seven habits of highly effective people.* New York: Simon & Schuster.

Cowan, N. (2001). The magical number 4 in short-term memory: A reconsideration of mental storage capacity. *Behavioral and Brain Sciences, 24,* 87–114.

Crannell, A. (1994). *Writing in mathematics with Dr. Annalisa Crannell* [Online]. Available: http://www.fandm.edu/Departments/Mathematics/writing_in_math/ writing_index.html

Crew, J. (1969, Spring). The effect of study strategies of the retention of college text material. *Journal of Reading Behavior, 1*(2), 45–52.

Crossland, R., & Clarke, B. (2002). *The leader's voice: How your communication can inspire action and get results!* New York: Select Books.

Crowley, K., & Siegler, R. (1999, March–April). Explanation and generalization in young children's strategy learning. *Child Development, 70*(2), 304–16.

Damasio, A. (1999). *The feeling of what happens.* New York: Harcourt Brace.

Danielson, C. (2002). *Enhancing student achievement.* Alexandria, VA: ASCD.

Darling-Hammond, L. (1997). *The right to learn: A blueprint for creating schools that work.* San Francisco: Jossey-Bass.

DeFina, P. (2003). *The neurobiology of memory: Understand, apply, and assess student memory.* Presentation at the Learning and the Brain Conference, Cambridge, MA.

Dewey, J. (1997). *How we think.* New York: Dover.

Dickman, M., & Blair, N. (2002). *Connecting the brain to leadership.* Thousand Oaks, CA: Corwin.

Dweck, C. (2000). *Self-theories: Their role in motivation, personality, and development.* Essays in Social Psychology. Philadelphia: Psychology Press.

Dye, L. (2000). Critical hours: Study shows why getting up too early may be counterproductive. *ABCnews.com* [Online]. Available: http://more.abcnews.go.com/sections/scitech/ dyehard/dyehard020703.html

Eichenbaum, H. (2003). *The neurobiology of learning and memory.* Paper presented at the Learning and the Brain Conference, Cambridge, MA.

Eliot, L. (1999). *What's going on in there?* New York: Bantam.

Engle, R. W., Kane, M. J., & Tuholski, S. W. (1999). Individual differences in working memory capacity and what they tell us about controlled attention, general fluid intelligence and functions of the prefrontal cortex. In A. Miyake & P. Shah (Eds.). *Models of working memory: Mechanisms of active maintenance and executive control* (pp. 102–131). Cambridge: Cambridge University Press.

Erlauer, L. (2003). *The brain-compatible classroom.* Alexandria, VA: ASCD.

Feinstein, S. (2004). *Secrets of the teenage brain.* San Diego, CA: Brain Store.

Fogarty, R. (1997). *Brain compatible classrooms.* Arlington Heights: SkyLight.

Gamon, D., & Bragdon, A. (2001). *Learn faster and remember more.* South Yarmouth, MA: Bragdon.

Gardner, H. (1983). *Frames of mind: The theory of multiple intelligences.* New York: Basic Books.

Gazzaniga, M. (1999). *The mind's past*. Berkeley: University of California Press.

Gelb, M. (1998). *How to think like Leonardo da Vinci*. New York: Dell.

Giannetti, C., & Sagarese, M. (2001). *Cliques*. New York: Broadway.

Giedd, J. (2002). Inside the teenage brain. *Frontline*. Boston: Public Broadcasting Service.

Glasser, W. (1999). *Choice theory*. New York: Perennial.

Goldberg, E. (2001). *The executive brain: Frontal lobes and the civilized mind*. New York: Oxford University Press.

Goleman, D. (1995). *Emotional intelligence*. New York: Bantam.

Goleman, D. (1998). *Working with emotional intelligence*. New York: Bantam.

Goleman, D., Boyatzis, R., & McKee, A. (2002). *Primal leadership*. Boston: Harvard Business School Press.

Good study habits and academic performance: Findings from the NAEP 1994 U.S. History and Geography Assessments. (1997). Vol. 2(4) [Online]. Available: http://nces.ed.gov/pubs97/web/97931.asp

Gordon, B., & Berger, L. (2003). *Intelligent memory*. New York: Viking.

Graf, P., & Schacter, D. L. (1985). Implicit and explicit memory for new associations in normal subjects and amnesic patients. *Journal of Experimental Psychology: Learning, Memory, and Cognition, 11*, 501–518.

Graham, R. (1999).Unannounced quizzes raise test scores selectively for mid-range students. *Teaching of Psychology, 26*(4), 271–273.

Halber, D. (2003). Basal ganglia are brain's Dr. Jekyll and Mr. Hyde. *MIT Tech Talk, 47*(23).

Hamann, S. B., Ely, T., Grafton, S., & Kilts, C. (1999). Amygdala activity related to enhanced memory for pleasant and aversive stimuli. *Nature Neuroscience, 2*, 289–293.

Harvey, S., & Goudvis, A. (2000). *Strategies that work*. York, ME: Stenhouse.

Hattie, J. (1999, August 2). *Influences on student learning*. Inaugural lecture, professor of education, University of Auckland [Online]. Available: http://www.arts.auckland.ac.nz/edu/staff/jhattie/Inaugural.html

Higbee, K. (1996). *Your memory: How it works and how to improve it*. New York: Marlowe.

Jacobs, H. (1997). *Curriculum mapping*. Alexandria, VA: ASCD.

Jensen, E. (1998). *Teaching with the brain in mind*. Alexandria, VA: ASCD.

Jensen, E. (2001). *Arts with the brain in mind*. Alexandria, VA: ASCD.

Johnson, D. (2001). *Critical issue: Beyond social promotion and retention—Five strategies to help students succeed* [Online]. Available: http://www.ncrel.org/sdrs/areas/issues/students/atrisk/at800.htm

Johnson, D., Johnson R., & Holubec, E. (1994). *New circles of learning: cooperation in the classroom and school*. Alexandria, VA: ASCD.

Johnson, G. (2000, April 21). Learning requires sleep. *St. Louis Post-Dispatch*.

Johnson, N. (1995). *Active questioning*. Beavercreek, OH: Pieces of Learning.

Johnson, S., Baxter, L., Wilder, L., Pipe. J., Heiserman, J., & Prigatano, G. (2002). Neural correlates of self-reflection. *Brain, 125*, 1808–1814.

Kahn, P. (2002). *Advice on using examples of ideas* [Online]. Palgrave Macmillan Ltd., Houndmills, Basingstoke, Hampshire, RG21 6XS, England. Available: http://www.palgrave.com/skills4study/html/subject_areas/maths/maths_ideas.htm

Keeley, M. (1997). *The basics of effective learning*. Unpublished manuscript, Bucks County College [Online]. Available: http://www.bucks.edu/~specpop/memory.htm

Kemmis, S. (1985). Action research and the politics of reflection. In D. Boud, R. Keogh, & D. Walker (Eds.). *Reflection: Turning nursing into learning*. London: Kogan Page.

Kenyon, G. (2002). Mind mapping can help dyslexics. *BBC News* [Online]. Available: http://news.bbc.co.uk/1/hi/education/1926739.stm

Kerry, S. (2002). Memory and retention time. *Educationreform.net* [Online]. Available: http://www.education-reform.net/memory.htm

Klein, K., & Boals, A. (2001). Expressive writing can increase working memory capacity. *Journal of Experimental Psychology: General, 130*, 520–533.

Kohn, A. (1993). *Punished by rewards*. New York: Houghton Mifflin.

LeDoux, J. (2002). *Synaptic self*. New York: Viking.

Leonard, J. (2004). What are essential questions and how are they created? *The Ihouse* [Online]. Available: http://www.lth3.k12.il.us/inquiryhouse/index.htm.

Levine, M. (2002). *A mind at a time*. New York: Simon & Schuster.

Levine, M. (2003). *The myth of laziness*. New York: Simon & Schuster.

Lewis, T., Amini, B., & Lannon, R. (2000). *A general theory of love*. New York: Random House.

Loveless, T. (2003). *The Brown Center report on American education*. Washington, DC: Brookings Institution.

Marzano, R. (1992). *A different kind of classroom: Teaching with dimensions of learning*. Alexandria, VA: ASCD.

Marzano, R. (1998). *A theory based meta-analysis of research on instruction*. Aurora, CO: Mid-continent Regional Educational Laboratory.

Marzano, R. J., Pickering, D. J., Norford, J., Paynter, D., & Gaddy, B. (2001). *A handbook for classroom instruction that works*. Alexandria, VA: ASCD.

Marzano, R. J., Pickering, D. J., & Pollack, J. (2001). *Classroom instruction that works*. Alexandria, VA: ASCD.

Maslow, A., & Lowery, R. (Eds.). (1998). *Toward a psychology of being* (3rd ed.). New York: Wiley.

Mason, D., & Kohn, M. (2001). *The memory workbook*. Oakland, CA: New Harbinger.

Mateika, J., Millrood, D., & Mitru. G. (2002). The impact of sleep on learning and behavior in adolescents. *Teachers College Record, 104*(4), 704–726.

Merriam-Webster collegiate dictionary. (1993). 10th ed. Springfield, MA: Merriam-Webster.

National Education Association. (2003). *Balanced assessment: The key to accountability and improved student learning* [Online]. Available: http://www.assessmentinst.com/pdfs/nea-balancedassess.pdf

Northwest Regional Educational Laboratory (NWREL). (2002). *Research you can use to improve results* [Online]. Originally prepared by Kathleen Cotton, NWREL, Portland, OR, and published by ASCD in 1999. Available: http://www.nwrel.org/scpd/re-engineering/rycu/index.shtml

O'Connor, K. (1999). *How to grade for learning*. Arlington Heights, IL: Skylight.

Ogle, D. (1986). The K-W-L: A teaching model that develops active reading of expository text. *The Reading Teacher, 39,* 564–570.

Olivier, C., & Bowler, R. (1996). *Learning to learn.* New York: Fireside.

Paul, R. (1993). *Critical thinking: How to prepare students for a rapidly changing world.* Santa Rosa, CA: Foundation for Critical Thinking.

Payne, R. (2001). *A framework for understanding poverty.* Highlands, TX: Aha Process Inc.

Performance Management. (1994). *Feedback is critical to improving performance.* Washington, DC: Office of Personnel Management.

Perkins, D. (1995). *Outsmarting IQ.* New York: Free Press.

Perry, B. (2000, November). How the brain learns best. *Instructor Magazine* [Online]. Available: http://teacher.scholastic.com/professional/bruceperry/brainlearns.htm

Peterson, S. (2000). *The nature of the young brain: How the young brain learns* [Cassette recording]. Alexandria, VA: ASCD.

Pinker, S. (1999). *How the mind works.* New York: Norton.

Popham, W. J. (2001). *The truth about testing: An educator's call to action.* Alexandria, VA: ASCD.

Quartz, S., & Sejnowski, T. (2002). *Liars, lovers, and heroes: What the new brain science reveals about how we become who we are.* New York: HarperCollins.

Rabinowitz, J. C., & Craik, F. I. M. (1986). Specific enhancement effects associated with word generation. *Journal of Memory and Language, 25,* 226–237.

Ratey, J. (2001). *A user's guide to the brain.* New York: Pantheon.

Restak, R. (2000). *Mysteries of the mind.* Washington, DC: National Geographic.

Richards, R. (2003). *The source for learning & memory strategies.* East Moline, IL: Linguisystems.

Rodgers, C. (2002, June). Defining reflection: Another look at John Dewey and reflective thinking. *Teachers College Record, 104*(4), 842–866.

Rogers, S., Ludington, J., & Graham, S. (1997). *Motivation and learning.* Evergreen, CO: Peak Learning Systems.

Rowe, M. B. (1973). *Teaching science as continuous inquiry.* New York: McGraw-Hill.

Rowe, M. B. (1986). Wait time: Slowing down may be a way of speeding up. *Journal of Teacher Education, 37*(1), 43–50.

Sapolsky, R. (1998). *Why zebras don't get ulcers.* New York: W. H. Freeman.

Schacter, D. (1996). *Searching for memory.* New York: Basic Books.

Schacter, D. (2001). *The seven sins of memory.* New York: Houghton Mifflin.

Schenck, J. (2000). *Learning, teaching and the brain.* Thermopolis, WY: Knowa.

Schmoker, M. (1999). *Results: The key to continuous school improvement* (2nd ed.). Alexandria, VA: ASCD.

Senge, P., Cambron-McCabe, N., Lucas, T., Smith, B., Dutton, J., & Kleiner, A. (2000). *Schools that learn.* New York: Doubleday.

Sevener, D. (1990, January). Retention: More malady than therapy. *Synthesis, 1*(1), 1–4.

Shaywitz, S. (2003). *Overcoming dyslexia.* New York: Knopf.

Siegel, D. (1999). *The developing mind.* New York: Guildford.

Singer-Freeman, K. (2003). *Working memory capacity. Preliminary results of research in progress.* Unpublished manuscript, Purchase College, State University of New York [Online]. Available: http://www.ns.purchase.edu/psych/faculty/freeman.html

Small, G. (2002). *The memory bible.* New York: Hyperion.

Sousa, D. (2001). *How the brain learns.* Thousand Oaks, CA: Corwin.

Sousa, D. (2002). *Is brain research making any difference in school* [Cassette recording]. From Summer Learning Brain Expo, Audio Visual Education Network.

Sousa, D. (2003). *How the gifted brain learns.* Thousand Oaks, CA: Corwin.

Sprenger, M. (1999). *Learning and memory: The brain in action.* Alexandria, VA: ASCD.

Sprenger, M. (2002). *Becoming a wiz at brain-based teaching.* Thousand Oaks, CA: Corwin.

Sprenger, M. (2003). *Differentiation through learning styles and memory.* Thousand Oaks, CA: Corwin.

Squire, L., & Kandel, E. (1999). *Memory: From mind to molecules.* New York: Scientific American Library.

Stahl, R. J. (1994). *Using think-time and wait-time skillfully in the classroom.* ERIC Abstracts, report number EDO-SO-94-3.

Sternberg, R., Grigorenko, E., & Jarvin, L. (2001, March). Improving reading instruction: The triarchic model. *Educational Leadership, 58*(6).

Stickgold, R., Whidbee, D., Schirmer, B., Patel, V., & Hobson, J. (2000). Visual discrimination task improvement: A multi-step process occurring during sleep. *Journal of Cognitive Neuroscience, 12*(2).

Stiggins, R. (2001). *Student involved classroom assessment* (3rd ed.). Columbus, OH: Merrill–Prentice Hall.

Stronge, J. (2002). *Qualities of effective teachers.* Alexandria, VA: ASCD.

Thomas, A. (2000). London cabbies more than the full quid. *News in Science* [Online]. Available: http://www.abc.net.au/science/news/stories/s110277.htm

Tileston, D. (2000). *Ten best teaching practices.* Thousand Oaks, CA: Corwin.

Tileston, D. (2004). *What every teacher should know about effective teaching strategies.* Thousand Oaks, CA: Corwin.

Tobin, K. (1987, Spring). The role of wait time in higher cognitive level learning. *Review of Educational Research, 57*(1), 69–95.

Tomlinson, C. (1999). *The differentiated classroom: Responding to the needs of all learners.* Alexandria, VA: ASCD.

Tovani, C. (2000). *I read it but I don't get it: Comprehension strategies for adolescent readers.* Portland, ME: Stenhouse.

Tuckman, B. W. (1998). Using tests as an incentive to motivate procrastinators to study. *Journal of Experimental Education, 66,* 141–147.

Tulving, E. (1985). How many memory systems are there? *American Psychologist, 40,* 385–398.

Tulving, E. (1999). Episodic vs. semantic memory. In R. Wilson & F. Keil (Eds.). *The MIT encyclopedia of the cognitive sciences.* Cambridge, MA: MIT Press.

Vacha, E., & McBride, M. (1993, March). Cramming: A barrier to student success, a way to beat the system, or an effective learning strategy? *College Student Journal, 27*(1), 2–11.

Viadero, D. (2003, October 8). Homework not on rise, studies find. *Education Week*, 23(6), 16.

Wellington, B. (1996). Orientations to reflective practice. *Educational Research*, 38(3), 307–315.

Wenglinsky, H. (2002, February 13). How schools matter: The link between teacher classroom practices and student academic performance. *Education Policy Analysis Archives*, 10(12) [Online]. Available: http://epaa.asu.edu/epaa/v10n12/

Wheatley, M. (2004). *Simple conversations*. Presentation at the ASCD Annual Conference, New Orleans.

Whitaker, J. (1999). *The memory solution*. New York: Avery.

Wiggins, G., & McTighe, J. (1998). *Understanding by design*. Alexandria, VA: ASCD.

Williamson, A. (1997, July). Reflection in adult learning with particular reference to learning-in-action. *Australian Journal of Adult and Community Education*, 37(2), 93–99.

Wong, H., & Wong, R. (1991). *The first days of school*. Sunnyvale, CA: Wong.

Zola, S. (2002). *Brain-based memory in the classroom*. Presentation at the Learning Brain Expo, San Diego, CA.

Zull, J. (2002). *The art of changing the brain*. Sterling, VA: Stylus.

Index

Note: Page numbers followed by the letter *f* indicate figures.

About the Author

Marilee Sprenger is a professional development consultant who has taught at all levels, from pre-kindergarten to graduate school. She is an adjunct professor at Aurora University where she teaches brain-compatible strategies and memory courses. For the past 15 years she has been engaged in raising student achievement using brain-based teaching strategies, differentiation, and memory research. She is a member of the American Academy of Neurology, the Cognitive Neuroscience Society, and the Learning and Brain Society, as well as many education organizations such as ASCD and Phi Delta Kappa. Sprenger's recent publications include: *Learning and Memory: The Brain in Action* published by ASCD, *Becoming a Wiz at Brain-based Teaching* published by Corwin Press, and *Differentiation through Learning Styles and Memory* also published by Corwin. She has written numerous articles and provides staff development internationally. She assists schools and regions across the continent in translating and applying current neuroscience research, cognitive science research, and scientifically based educational research.

You can reach her at 5820 Briarwood Lane, Peoria, IL 61614. Phone: (309) 692-5820. E-mail: msprenge@aol.com. (Note that there is no "r" at the end of her e-mail username.) Her Web site is brainlady.com.

Related ASCD Resources: The Brain and Learning

At the time of publication, the following ASCD resources were available; for the most up-to-date information about ASCD resources, go to www.ascd.org. ASCD stock numbers are noted in parentheses.

Multimedia

The Human Brain Professional Inquiry Kit by Bonnie Benesh (#999003)

Networks

Visit the ASCD Web site (http://www.ascd.org) and search for "networks" for information about professional educators who have formed groups around various topics, including "Brain-Compatible Learning." Look in the "Network Directory" for current facilitators' addresses and phone numbers.

Online Courses

Go to ASCD's Home Page (http://www.ascd.org) and click on professional development to find the following ASCD Professional Development Online Courses: *The Brain: Memory and Learning Strategies* and *The Brain: Understanding the Mind.*

Print Products

Educational Leadership November 1998 "How the Brain Learns" (#198261)
Brain-Based Learning Electronic Topic Pack (#197194)
Brain Matters: Translating Research into Classroom Practice by Patricia Wolfe (#101004)
Education on the Edge of Possibility by Geoffrey Caine and Renate Nummela Caine (#19702)
Learning & Memory: The Brain in Action by Marilee Sprenger (#199213)
Teaching to the Brain's Natural Learning Systems by Barbara K. Givens (#101075)
Teaching with the Brain in Mind (2nd ed.) by Eric Jensen (#104013)

Videotapes

The Brain and Learning (4 videos) (#498062)
The Brain and Mathematics (2 videos) (#400237)
The Brain and Reading (3 videos) (#499207)

For more information, visit us on the World Wide Web (http://www.ascd.org), send an e-mail message to member@ascd.org, call the ASCD Service Center (1-800-933-ASCD or 703-578-9600, then press 2), send a fax to 703-575-5400, or write to Information Services, ASCD, 1703 N. Beauregard St., Alexandria, VA 22311-1714, USA.